MW00935463

BUT GOD!!!

BUT GOD!!!

Robinson, Debbie Pearl River, LA

XULON PRESS

Xulon Press
2301 Lucien Way #415
Maitland, FL 32751
407.339.4217
www.xulonpress.com

© 2022 by Robinson, Debbie Pearl River, LA

All rights reserved solely by the author. The author
guarantees all contents are original and do not infringe upon
the legal rights of any other person or work. No part of this
book may be reproduced in any form without the permission
of the author.

Due to the changing nature of the Internet, if there are any web
addresses, links, or URLs included in this manuscript, these
may have been altered and may no longer be accessible. The
views and opinions shared in this book belong solely to the
author and do not necessarily reflect those of the publisher.
The publisher therefore disclaims responsibility for the views
or opinions expressed within the work.

Unless otherwise indicated, Scripture quotations taken from
the King James Version (KJV) – *public domain.*

Paperback ISBN-13: 978-1-6628-5493-4
Ebook ISBN-13: 978-1-6628-5494-1

Table of Contents

PRELUDE

For those who've had tearstained pillows, sighed word-less prayers, felt like the breath was kicked out of you, cried until you could cry no more, fought your way back from the pit of despair and those still wondering through the valley.
Keep the faith…
God is there….
Even when your tears blur your view!!!

We all have our days where we feel we can't survive. Sometimes dreams are shattered. Friendships may fall apart. Loved ones may hurt us. Finances may worry us. Sickness may overtake us. We may even lose people we love. But, GOD will ALWAYS be there to guide us through even the toughest times. Never lose FAITH!!!

You may not have been through the same things I've been through. However, I have experienced the same shock, the same anger, the same depression. I have struggled with unforgiveness, and the inability to let go. I, too, have wondered if I will ever recover – ever trust again, begin again, and be able to move on. Yes, I have been there. But thanks to the grace of God, I am no longer there. I pray this book will give you hope.

I am a living witness to the fact that God is able. Not only to comfort you, but to bring you through your present brokenness. He will take the broken pieces of your heart and fashion them into an incredible vessel of priceless value. He can rebuild your spirit and make you whole again. He's able to turn every scar into a beauty mark that others admire. If you're wondering if you will ever be whole again… You can be!!!

As I tell my life story, my hope is that it will be a testimony to someone. I pray it will help someone see that even when life seems to keep knocking you down, if you continue to hold onto Jesus, he will walk with you every step of the way and through it all.

Your life can be beautiful, even with all the ups and downs. Regardless of how you were raised, you CAN break the chain of abuse, alcoholism, infidelity and anything else. I chose to break the chain and God has blessed me tremendously. He has blessed me with a wonderful, beautiful family, all living and working for him.

ABOUT THE AUTHOR

The author shares her personal testimony in this memoir to encourage readers to "continue to hold onto Jesus... even when life seems to keep knocking you down." Mrs. Robinson writes about her life in chronological order, highlighting difficult and devastating moments in which she turned to God for strength and support. The author's inspirational memoir provides "witness to the fact that God is able, not only to comfort you, but to bring you through your present brokenness.

Mrs. Robinson lives in Louisiana with her husband. She has 3 children and 7 grandchildren who are all living for God and ministering in his kingdom. Mrs. Robinson plays piano and substitutes leading worship when the full time worship leader is away. She also teaches Sunday School. She has taught Sunday School over 50 years. She and her husband were involved in Sunday School Evangelism and Bus Ministry in various churches for 35 years. Her greatest joy is her God, her Children, Grandchildren, Friends, Husband, Church family and Family. All of her children and grandchildren, who are old enough, are involved in ministry in one way or the other. Some pastor a church, some teach, most are in music ministry, some are in servitude and some are in church administration. As you read her story you will be amazed at what God has done.

IN THE BEGINNING

I was born in 1953, in Paragould Arkansas. My mom told me Dad dropped her off at a clinic there then picked her and me up a few days later.

We lived in the country, right outside of Sedgwick, Arkansas. Our house was a big old place with a screened in porch that stretched the width of the house in front and back. We didn't have an inside toilet so we always had a chamber pot on the back porch to use at night. Each morning it was dumped in the outhouse, rinsed out and placed back on the porch. We also did not have running water. We had to prime the water pump outside each morning. So, we had to make sure there was a container of water handy to prime it with.

Debbie!!! Deborah!!! Hurry, get out here!!! Your dad is choking to death!!! This is the first real memory I have.

My dad had come home drunk, which was pretty much an everyday occurrence. He was worse off than normal on this particular night. It was very late. He was in the house just a while when he got very sick at his stomach. He went to the front porch, laid down with his head hanging off the porch, holding the screen door open with one hand, and proceeded to throw his guts up. He was out there quite a long time. So, my mother went to check on him and discovered he had passed out and the screen door had closed on his neck. He was choking. His face was turning blue. Mom hollered for me to come hold the screen door while she tried to get him up. She pulled with all her might but could not budge him. So she put my two sisters in the car and went into town to get my uncles to come help. She told me I would have to stand there and hold the door off his neck. She said if I let it go he could die. I remember being so scared standing there all by myself out in the boonies, holding that door. The door was very heavy. My arm hurt terribly from the pressure. I shook from the pain. I could see animal eyes shining in the woods across the road and hear all the noises that come alive at night. I was crying because I truly thought Dad was dying. It is still such a vivid memory of being one of the scariest times in my life. I was about five at the time. It was such a young age to be left alone in the middle of the night. ("But God"!!!). His loving arms were wrapped around me and he watched over me. Mom made it back along with my uncles. It took them a very long time to get him up and settled. They finally got Dad cleaned up and in bed. They stayed the night just in case they were needed.

A funny memory I have from that old house was, when my dad came home from a squirrel hunting trip one day. He had shot several squirrels. When he got home he threw them on the back porch to clean later. We had a house full of company. My sister, Tina, who was about four years old went to the back porch to use the restroom in the chamber pot. When she was finished she couldn't find the bath tissue. She hollered and hollered for someone to help her, but there was so much noise in the house, no one heard her. So, she proceeded to use one of the squirrels tail to wipe her bottom. When she came back into the house she kept squirming and scratching her behind. This was embarrassing our mom. So, after a while mom took her into the bedroom and discovered the reason for Tina's squirming and scratching. Needless to say it wasn't easy getting all the tiny prickly squirrel hairs off her bottom.

Dad was a gentle and kind guy, who loved to laugh, until he started drinking. When he started drinking he turned into a completely different man. Dad never beat us but he beat Mom. Then she would take her frustration out on us, especially me, since I was the oldest. So, it was nothing for me to have a busted lip, black eye, or bruises. ("But God")!!! Most of my memories from those days was a cycle of Dad coming home drunk, him and Mom fighting, which sometimes led to him beating her, and then later her beating me.

I have fond memories of our grandparents. Our grandparents on my dad's side had a huge house up on blocks. No telling what you might find under that house. It might be chickens, pigs, dogs, cats, or a big ole snake. I remember my grandmother getting a chicken from the chicken coop, grabbing it by the head, swinging it around and around, popping its neck, the head coming off and the chicken running all over the yard, headless, with blood squirting everywhere, until it died. When it finally died, grandma would pick him up, pluck all the feathers, wash him, cut him up and we would all sit down to an awesome fried chicken dinner later in the day. My granddad was an old man. But, that didn't stop him from getting drunk and stumbling around all over the place. He was always kind to us. My grandmother would sit in an old rocking chair and spit tobacco into a spittoon.

The only real memory of my grandparents on my mom's side was my grandmother was always kind of cranky, but my grandfather was very gentle. He had a little apple orchard in the back of their house. He would sit on the porch and cut slices of apples for us to eat, as he told us stories.

To make a living our whole family would chop or pick cotton and any other type jobs. As soon as we were old enough we were in the cotton field. I was around five years old when I started working in the field. When I got to the end of the row and my sack was full, I didn't have the strength to lift it up onto the scale hook to get it weighed. One of the men in the truck would jump down and lift it for me. Then, once it was weighed he would empty it and hand it back to me. Throughout my life God seemed to always put little kindnesses like that for me. I remember reaching down to pull a bow of cotton and a huge black spider was sitting on top of the bow. Things like that and having to go to the bathroom in the woods and watch for snakes at the same time was very scary. ("But God"!!!) His hand of protection was always there.

During this same period of my life my finger was nearly cut off. Our parents were gone and our older cousin was at our house with us one day. She wanted to wash our hair. So, since there were no inside bathrooms she was doing it outside by the water pump. We had a huge old wheelbarrow. So, we all got in the wheelbarrow, filled it with water, like a swimming pool, and one by one jumped out to get our hair washed. We were having a fun time. When it was my turn, I stood on the edge of the wheelbarrow and boom, it turned over. We all went flying out. We were all on the ground laughing. I didn't realize anything was wrong until I brought my hand up to my mouth and saw the blood squirting from my finger. It was dangling, barely attached and looked like ground hamburger meat. I didn't feel the pain at first because it had severed all the nerves. Shortly after that, I became faint and don't remember a lot of how we got help or got to the hospital and all that. The next thing I remember is my hand all bandaged and the doctor telling my mom that I could still lose it. It was touch and go. The doctor said I had to be extremely careful. Thankfully it healed well and they didn't have to cut it completely off. It is deformed and the nail doesn't grow right on it but I still have use of it and I thank God for that. ("But God"!!!) Once again God had his hand on me.

One time my Dad let me go fishing with him and a couple friends. I had begged and begged to go and he finally let me. To get to the fishing hole we had to walk through knee high brush and briar. By the time we got there my legs were all scratched, bleeding and hurting. There were a couple big logs under a tree. I sat down on one of the logs. After Dad got his fishing line in the water he sat down on a log across from me. Suddenly he hollered, grabbed my arm and jerked me off the log I was sitting on. About that time a huge snake fell out of the tree, right where I had been sitting. One of the men shot it. I just stood there shaking. That snake would have fallen right on me. It still gives me chills when I think about it. ("But God"!!!)

The school I went to was a two room building. There was no kindergarten. The first, second, third and fourth graders were in one room and the fifth, sixth, seventh and eighth graders were in another.

My grandfather got tuberculosis. I had no idea what that was since I was only six years old. Some of the older kids at school were so cruel and teased me about my grandfather having to go away to an institution because he had TB. One girl said "I don't want to sit by Debbie, her grandpa has TB". I cried and cried because I thought it was some sort of dirty issue. In just a few months Grandpa was healed and released from the institution. ("But God"!!!) I'm so thankful for his healing power.

When I was seven our parents bought some land and started building our first home from the ground up. We were actually going to have an inside toilet. We got a brand new coal stove to cook on and warm the house. I was so excited when we finally got to move in. The bathroom was not finished so we still had to use the outhouse. There was a few other area's not quite finished but we were still able to move in. I loved that little house. It was so nice and had all the newest furniture and all. I just knew things were going to be better. Dad was going to stop drinking and beating Mom and she was going to stop beating me.

We had been in our new home for just a couple months when suddenly our parents told us we were moving to California, where Dad's half brother and his family lived. I had never met them. I was so shocked. I remember crying my eyes out as we left our home that had so much promise, but still wasn't even finished. I recently asked my dad right before he passed away why we moved in the middle of building our home and when everything seemed so good. He said because he lost his job and couldn't find another one. Supposedly California was the land of opportunity and jobs were plentiful. Dad had very little education. He couldn't read or write. His jobs were basically mechanic, handyman, field worker, service station, and construction type jobs. He was a hard worker though. I would see him stay out until the bars closed at 2:00 AM and still get up around 6:00 AM and be at work on time. So, we sold everything, packed our car and headed to an unknown place. We said goodbye to our grandparents, cousins, friends and life as we had known it. Our lives were about to drastically change.

California

I will never forget the sadness I felt as we waved goodbye to the only people I had ever known. The backseat of the car was loaded all the way up to the windows. We kids slept on top of the pile. There was no room to sit so we laid all the way there. It was so uncomfortable. I cried most of the way because I did not want to leave our family and friends. I think I knew our lives were about to change forever.

Moving from Arkansas, where there are lots of trees and greenery most all year long, to California was a shock. All we had heard was how beautiful California was. I'll never forget as we entered California and the Mojave desert. It was brown and ugly country. Sand as far as the eye could see. The main thing I remember is my mom crying as we drove across the country to Bakersfield. I don't remember much about our arrival, except feeling so lost in a place so foreign to us, and not a soul I had ever seen before.

My cousin Faye, who we called our aunt, because she was years older than us went to a great church there. Not long after our arrival we started going to church with her. I received the Holy Ghost and that has been my saving grace through all the years. I was only seven years old but God was living inside of me and he gave me the power and the strength to overcome anything. If it wasn't for the Lord, where would I be? ("But God"!!!) He has been so good to me and carried me through so many test and trials.

Not long after moving, Dad got a job on a farm. A three bedroom house came with the job. So, we lived in the country in a little house with fields and farm equipment all around us. We always referred to it as, Sam and Dee Bells place. They were the owners of the farm.

The nearest little town was about 10 miles from our home. It was a little country community called Pond. Pond consisted of a little grocery store, gas station and an elementary school called Pond Elementary.

Mom got a job working at the City Hall in the town of Wasco. Wasco was about 20 miles from Pond. By this time I was 8 years old. We kids had to walk down the dirt road each day to catch the bus. It was horrible when it rained. By the time we got to the bus stop we were soaking wet and a muddy mess. Mom and Dad both left early each morning. So, it was my job to make sure each kid was dressed, and out the door on time. Our parents were gone from early morning until late evening. Many times Dad didn't come home until two or three in the morning. As soon as he got off work he would head to the bar or one of his most recent girlfriends homes.

I remember being so lonely, especially in the summertime. We could not watch TV. Dad had a TV in the living room, but we were not allowed to go in there when the TV was on. One day, in the summertime a little girl from our church came home with us to spend a couple of days. She saw the TV and wanted to turn it on. I told her we couldn't and to leave it alone. However, she turned it on anyway. When she turned it on, there was a little cartoon called Mighty Mouse. She and both of my sisters sat down and watched it for about five minutes. I ran over and turned the TV off. I was so scared. I just knew hell was going to open up and swallow us right then and there. That little girl went home and told her parents that she watched TV at our house. The next church service our Pastor got up and told the entire church to never let their children come to our home. He said there were things in our home that was bad and he didn't want the other church children exposed. We were so devastated and embarrassed. ("But God"!!!) He comforted us.

There was a big pasture across the field from our house. I don't remember what grew there but each year sheep herders would come with their flock of sheep and stay for days while the sheep cleared the field. The herders could not speak English but just having someone close was so exciting to us. Even though they did not know our language we were able to communicate. One of their dogs had puppies and they gave us one. We all loved that dog.

He was a German Shepherd. He would nip at my brother's heels and when my brother would cry, Dad would ask him "did he bite you?" Dad was very country so he ran all his words together. Therefore the "did he bite you" came out "Diddybitechee?" That became the dog's name. For a few years, Diddybitechee was part of our family and gave us so much pleasure. He fought off coyotes, and helped keep snakes and other varmints away. One morning we got up and called and called for him but he did not come. We found him under the cotton trailer. He was dead. He was all mangled from a wolf, coyote or something that was bigger and stronger than he was. We kids mourned that old dog something fierce. ("But God"!!!) He mends the broken hearted.

For some reason Dad bought a big old ram. He was placed in a fenced area. That crazy ram got out of the fence more times than I want to remember. He always would charge us. We were scared to death of that thing with those big curled horns. One day we started off to school and my youngest sister Jackie was in a horrible mood and already crying before we ever left the house. We were running late and I was afraid we would not get to the bus stop in time. As we took off walking we saw the ram was out of his pen. I picked up a big stick and told the kids to stay behind me. Our dog was running around and barking like crazy. He ran right through Jackie's legs and knocked her off her feet. She landed on her behind. So, here I was with a big stick trying to keep the ram away and trying to console Jackie and keep the other kids safe. I was so mad at my dad by then. However, I wound up banging the sticks together, throwing rocks and anything else that I could, to keep the ram away until we got back in the house. We then had to call Mom and tell her we had missed the bus. Boy was she mad. Thankfully she didn't beat me that time. ("But God"!!!)

The beatings became worse. Dad would work all day and then go to the bars. We never knew when he would show up at home. He had affair after affair. When he did come home, he and Mom fought and he would wind up beating her much of the time. I think the pressure of work, being away from family and what Mom had to put up with from Dad, was just so much on her, that she unfortunately took it out on us. Mainly me, since I was the oldest.

At nine years old my job was to make sure the house was spotless, beds made, bathrooms cleaned, floors swept, mopped and waxed, clothes washed, ironed and put away. Tina's job was to wash dishes. If Tina didn't feel like washing dishes she would hide them in the empty spaces, above the top kitchen cabinets. We were missing lots of utensils. One day Mom was on a ladder and found the lost dishes where Tina hid them. Tina got a really hard spanking but I don't remember any bruises and so on. Our little brother and sister, Jackie and Mike, had no responsibilities. I guess because they were only three and four at the time.

Mom was very strict about the house. Everything had to be perfect. We had these old dark green tile floors that you had to mop and wax. Living in the middle of a dirt field was horrible. Every time you went outside, if you didn't wipe your feet good you would leave white dirt tracked all over the floor. That made Mom furious. Each piece of furniture better not have a speck of dust on it either. If everything was not clean to perfection or if the clothes were not perfectly washed and ironed when she got home, I would get the beating of my life. If the dishes were not done right Tina got beat. So, after I cleaned each morning I would get all the sheets out of the closet and lay them on all the floors to catch any dirt the kids might track in. Around 5:30 each day, we would watch for the dirt rising from the road and knew it was Mom coming home. At that point we would gather up all the sheets and throw them in the closet. I was so scared every day. So, I would pretend I needed to use the bathroom, until she was in the house and I could brace myself for whatever mood she was in. If it had been a decent day at work and the house was to her liking, I knew I could safely come out of the bathroom. If the day had not gone well or if something was not to her liking, I would brace myself for the beating I knew was coming.

One Saturday she took a dress from Jackie's closet. For some reason she did not like the way Jackie's dress was ironed. She came storming into the room I was in and demanded I tell her I did not iron the dress. It was one of those ruffled, Martha Miniature dresses that was so hard to iron. One thing I can say for Mom is she always made sure we were well dressed. Anyway, when I told her I had indeed ironed the dress, she threw me down on the floor, sat on top of me and proceeded to use me for a punching bag. She quit hitting me long enough to say "you better tell me you did not iron this dress". I told her I would be lying if I said I didn't. So, she proceeded to use me for a punching bag over and over again. I don't know what made her finally quit. But, she eventually got off me and left me lying there. I got up and went to the bathroom and cleaned myself up. It was never mentioned again. I cried and cried. ("But God"!!!). I could feel God's loving arms around me. At times I would ask God to please just kill me. I would ask him to please just let me die.

One Sunday morning Mom told me to polish her shoes while she dressed my little brother Mike. She told me I better not get the polish on my dress. I had never polished shoes and never used one of those old corkscrew bottles with the round ball on the bottom. As I took the lid off, I couldn't get the stopper out. As I pulled harder, the cork gave way and polish splashed all over me. I cleaned everything up as best I could and silently cried knowing the minute she saw me, I was in for it. I cleaned all the polish off the cabinets and floor, but could not get it off my dress. When I realized it was futile to try to clean the spot off the dress anymore, I went into the room where she was. The minute she saw me, I literally saw her eyes turn red. She put Mike down on the bed and laid into me. I blocked out the actual beating. I just remember waking up with a bruised jaw, busted lip, bloody nose, black eye and pain. ("But God!!!") He spared me! My sisters tell me at some point I wet my pants. I cleaned myself up and we went on to church. When we got there she told anyone who asked what happened to me, that someone from school just walked up and started punching me. Now, you know those church people didn't believe that. I was nine years old for heaven sake. But, as many times as family and friends saw the after affects of beatings, no one ever intervened. Back then people just didn't.

Dad was always in the bars and many nights Mom would go looking for him. Sometimes she would take us with her and we would drive around town for hours trying to find which bar he was in. Sometimes we were left at home alone till late hours of the night. One time Mom and another lady went out looking for both their husbands and left all the kids at our house. It was really late at night and we were OK until one of the kids said they saw someone walking around the outside of our house. Then another kid said they saw someone smoking a cigarette out there. We lived way out in the country with no close neighbors. Of course each child's imagination began to run wild. It wasn't long until everyone was scared to death. My sister, Tina, went to the back closet and got a shotgun out of the closet. Two or three kids got knives from the kitchen drawer. One of the girls called the telephone operator and reported it. The operator said she would send a policeman out to our house. Right after that, Mom and the other lady came home. When we told them what was going on, they said we were foolish and in big trouble. Right then a police car pulled up in the front yard. Mom told all of us to run and jump in the bed and pretend like we were asleep. The police knocked on the door and said there had been a call from our house saying kids were left alone. Mom told him that wasn't possible because we had all been asleep for hours. The police asked if they could take a look in our bedrooms. They flashed their flashlights around our room. How we managed to pull it off is beyond me. However, we did and the police went on their way.

One day I had cleaned the house to perfection while the kids played outside. I had just waxed the floor when Jackie came in, tracking that old white dirt all across my clean floors. I knew I would get beat if it was like that when Mom got home so after Jackie tracked in several times, I locked her outside. She got mad and began to bang on the window. The window busted and cut her hand very deep. I grabbed a hand towel and tried to stop the bleeding. We ran outside and saw Dad driving down the road to change the irrigation water. We jumped, hollered and screamed until we got his attention. He jumped out of his truck and his eyes bugged out when he saw the blood everywhere. They took her to the hospital and got her hand stitched up. I just knew I was going to catch it when Mom got home. Dad really scolded me and had me in tears but unbelievably I didn't get beat that time.("But God"!!!)

The beatings always happened when Dad was not there. It was a horrible cycle. Dad would beat Mom and then when he wasn't there she would beat me and once in a while Tina, but never Jackie or Mike. Dad never laid a hand on us.

One time Dad was beating Mom and we thought he was going to kill her. We were all standing around them screaming but he wouldn't listen to us. My sister Tina was only seven but she went in the kitchen and got a butcher knife. I still don't know if she really intended to stab someone but when our dad saw her standing there with it, his eyes bugged out and he immediately stopped beating Mom and walked out of the room.

One night we got in the car to go to church and the car wouldn't start. Mom got out, opened the hood to find that Dad had taken the distributor cap off, to prevent us from going to church. Mom put the distributor cap back on. Dad came running out of the house mad as a hornet. Mom saw him and took off running down the road. He went running after her. I don't know if he deliberately pushed her down or if he tripped and they both fell. But, she came back to the car with her hands bleeding, pantyhose torn and her knees oozing blood. We didn't get to go to church that night. Things like this happened more than once. Dad just did not want us to go to church. One time, though, he kept asking us to stay home, but we went anyway and when we got home he had surprised us with a new piano. It was covered in white leather. I've never seen a white leather piano before or after that.

So many crazy things happened during that time of my life. One night my mom and aunt went looking for my dad and my uncle at the bars. My aunt was a very bold woman. You never knew what she was going to say or do. She would say anything that came to her mind. Especially if she was mad. While they were driving around she asked my mom to drive over to the African American side of town, to see if my dad and uncle were in the bars over there. Back then everything was still segregated. My dad was very prejudiced. The rest of the family was not. Mom told my aunt that there was no way my dad would ever be caught dead drinking in that area of town. But, she went ahead and drove over there. When we drove up to the bar, Dad was sitting in his truck with an African-American. My aunt jumped out of the truck, ran up there and started screaming at my dad. She used the (N) word several times. She said, " I thought you hated these people. All I ever hear you doing is run them down and talk about how much you hate them, and now here you are sitting in the truck drinking with one." Then, she ran in the bar and made a scene in there with my uncle. The whole time my mom was sitting in the car saying, " she's going to get us killed"!!!! ("But God"!!!) I personally could never understand someone being prejudice. God made each and every one of us. The Bible tells us he made us in his likeness. He died on the cross for all of our sins. Red, yellow, black or white, there's no difference to him and there's no difference to me.

Not long after that, my aunt once again embarrassed us. We were all in the car looking for my dad and my uncle, again. My mom drove out to a house of ill repute. When we drove up, men and women scattered. My aunt ran in the house. She caught my dad and uncle in bed with certain women, made a big scene then picked up someone's underwear and ran out on the front porch waving the underwear around hollering "who's are these?" She was screaming, hollering and calling all the women names. She told the men she saw there, that she was going to tell their wives. Then, suddenly people started threatening her. If I remember right, someone had a gun. She ran and jumped in our car. We hi-tailed it out of there. That was so scary, but funny too. ("But God"!!!) He kept his hand on us.

I went to Pond school from about the second grade until I graduated eighth grade. I was extremely shy when I first started. However, my fifth grade teacher, Mr. Clark, took me under his wings and told everyone he was going to get me out of my shyness, if it was the last thing he did. He started me singing with a recorded tape at the PTA meetings in front of everyone. Whenever there was a chance for him to make me do something to get me out of my shyness he would do it. By the time I was in seventh grade I was voted in as head cheerleader. Each student trying out for cheerleading had to try out and do a cheer, by themselves, in front of the entire school, and then the school voted. Only one cheerleader was picked and then that girl could pick her own cheerleading team. I could also pick our cheerleader attire. So, since I didn't wear shorts or pants, I chose culottes specially made with tops that had our school logo. All the other girls were OK with that. I became one of the most popular girls in school. I will never forget Mr. Clark. Many times I have wished I could find him. Just so I could thank him. Out of any adult, he made the biggest impact on my life.

One day we were playing crack the whip on the football field. I was one of the smaller kids in class. I was on the end of the whip and when we began to go faster and faster, the person holding my hand let go and I went flying down the football field. I landed on my shoulder and broke my collarbone. The bone was pushing my skin up to about chin level. The doctor asked me if I was a strong girl. Then, he put his hands on each side of my shoulder and shoved the bone back into place. I had to wear a brace for six weeks or so. ("But God"!!!) He protected me from getting my neck broke.

Right about this time Dad wound up running off with some woman and left us high and dry once again. We had to move to another little house down the road. My aunt wanted to get my mom out of the house for a while. So she invited Mom to go with her to a ladies conference in Bakersfield. They asked me to stay at my aunt's house and watch my two sisters and brother, plus my aunt's kids and a couple other kids. I was in fifth grade so I was around 10 or 11. To my surprise my uncle was there. He was in his bedroom watching TV. There was about 8 kids in the house. They were running all over the place. Dropping chips, drinks and whatever else all over the floor. They had made a huge mess. So, I grabbed a broom and started cleaning. I knew I would be in so much trouble if my mom and aunt came home to a filthy house. My uncle called all the kids into his room to watch a cartoon. I didn't think anything about it. So, as I was sweeping I proceeded to sweep in the bedroom where they all were. It was a mess. Popcorn and junk was all over the floor. When I scolded the kids for making such a mess they ran out of the room and I proceeded to finish cleaning up the mess. Not even thinking. When suddenly my uncle grabbed me, pulled me down onto the bed, put one hand over my mouth, held me down with his elbow and ran the other hand up under my blouse and bra, then up my shirt. I tried to fight him off but he was too strong. I kept hitting him with my fist and bawling my eyes out. But, it didn't faze him. He was a big man, about 6ft tall and around 230lbs. After awhile the kids came running back toward that end of the house so he let me go. I went in the bathroom and tried to clean myself up, washed my face and dried my tears. I went to the kitchen and just sat there until my Mom and aunt came home. I was numb. I was shaking like a leaf. I was too scared to tell anyone. I secretly cried for days and nights. One day he showed up at our house asking for me. My sister opened the door, and let him in. He looked at me and said he came to spend some time with me. I ran into the bedroom and locked the door. His coming to our house in the middle of the day showed me that was not a one time thing. I could not handle it anymore and told one of my friends. She immediately told her parents, but did not tell me she had told them. The following Wednesday night on the way to church, we drove up in front of my aunt and uncles house, instead of the church. There was two other cars parked there. In the cars were the parents of the other kids that were in the house that night and in one of the cars was our pastor and his wife. My mom got out of the car and got in the car with my pastor. One by one they had a child at a time get in the car and give an account of what happened that night. It was so strange. Because the other kids did not see what my uncle did. I wondered if he had done the same thing to someone else.

But when I ask questions no one would answer me. After the last kid got out of that car everyone drove home and it was never mentioned again. I was so hurt. My heart was breaking, but no one seemed to care. I was in total shock and could not understand why no one would talk about it or answer my questions. I now know why kids don't tell about things like this. Sometimes parents and others don't know how to deal with it. So, it is swept under the rug. Everyone continued on like it never happened. My uncle was always still around at all family events and so on. I kept my distance and stayed as far away as I could from him. I asked my mom about it years later and she acted like she didn't know what I was talking about. It bothers me to this day that apparently nothing was done.

Eighth grade graduation at Pond Elementary was a big deal. It was just like a high school graduation, except it was from eighth grade. I was so excited to be graduating with high honors. I was so proud and praised my God because I knew with my life at home it was only through him and Mr. Clark that I had done so good. In the middle of my graduation, right before the awards ceremony, I heard a loud commotion and turned around to see my drunk dad, stumbling down the isle, talking loudly, and making a scene, trying to find a place to sit. I was so embarrassed. Everyone was turning around to see what the commotion was and some just shaking their heads in disgust. But, I held my head high, walked across the stage and received my awards with Godly pride. ("But God")!!!! My Heavenly Father was right there walking with me.

Dad wound up moving back home and we later moved to a duck club. This was a place that rich people and movie stars came to hunt. There was a big old house with a bunkhouse attached. Also, there were cabins all around the house. Men stayed in the bunkhouse or in the cabins when they came to hunt. Our family's job was to take care of it all. We had to get up around 4 AM and cook breakfast for all the duck hunters and members. It was almost like a restaurant because we took orders, and so on. We had to have breakfast over in time for the men to make it to the duck blinds before sun up. My dad drove the men out to the blinds in a buckboard truck. At designated times throughout the day, Dad would drive around the duck ponds and pick up the men that had shot their limit or who were ready to come back to their cabin. Their ducks were tagged with their name and it was our job to pluck and clean the ducks and prepare them for safekeeping until the man headed home. The actor John Wayne was a member. Sometimes wives of the rich men would come with them. One time a lady and her husband had just been to Paris France and she brought all of us kids some candy from there. In the off-season Dad could do other odd jobs as long as he kept the club up in maintenance and so on. So, he bought several head of cattle. We had a couple horses for a short period and an old pig. We named the pig Oscar. Oscar was always making big holes in our yard to root in. He became our pet and it nearly killed us when Dad took him to be slaughtered. I don't know what happened to the horses. Dad took the cattle to auction. I got to go with him a couple times and really enjoyed it.

One day my sister Jacque and I were scuffling with each other and as I turned to swat at her, I realized I had just stepped over a snake. Right there in our bedroom was a great big king snake. Jacque and I just stood there staring at each other. Jacque was on one side of it and me on the other. Dad picked him up and put him outside. He said he would not kill it because it would keep the rattlesnakes and other things away.

We basically lived in the desert. So, there were a lot of rattlesnakes. We had to walk a mile and a fourth to catch the bus. Our brother Mike was in kindergarten and the bus dropped him off earlier than us. One day when he started walking home there was a huge rattlesnake stretched across the road. He was so scared. He crawled up on the fence and cried until eventually the snake crawled away. After that, my dad bought an old junk car for me to drive, only up and down that road. When Mike got off the bus he was supposed to sit in the car until we came home. So each day Mike would get off the bus about 1:00, then Jacque about 2:00, and they would wait in the car for me and Tina to get off our bus around 3:30. I would drive us home then and we would immediately start our chores. I still can't believe I was driving that young.

There was a family from Holland that moved down the road from us. They had a beautiful dog that had puppies. I don't know what kind of dog it was, but for some reason they gave me a puppy. They said his name was Beno and he was mine alone. I don't know what prompted that act of kindness from them. But, it still touches my heart to this day. I loved Beno. He was the only thing I had that was just mine. He grew quickly. Beno would always come running as fast as he could to greet us. For some reason he would dart in front of the car. Numerous times I would almost hit him but was able to always break just in time. I would scold him over and over. One terrible day he was either faster than normal or I was slower than normal and unfortunately I ran over him. All I could do was scream and cry. I could not believe that I had run over my own dog. My dad was nowhere around. My sisters ran in the house and called our mom. They were crying so hard she couldn't understand them. Later that day we buried him. We had a nice little ceremony for him. It took me awhile to get over that.

The duck club was a lot of work but for the first time since moving to California it felt like we were a real family. Mom still worked in town, but we were very far out in the country, and Dad stayed so busy he didn't have time to really drink and go to the bars and run around. We still got beat from time to time but since Dad was around most of the time we didn't get near as many beatings as before.

While we lived at the Duck Club my Uncle Jim, Aunt Gina and cousin Duane came for a visit from Arkansas. We all went to Disneyland. We had a wonderful week. Duane is several years younger than me. When he was younger I carried him around everywhere. We have always had a special bond. When he was little he was on his tricycle, underneath a tree, when a sudden thunder and lightning storm came up. Duane was struck by lightning. The doctors did not think he would live. ("But God"!!!). He healed Duane and has been with him all his life. He is the only cousin who has stayed in touch all these years.

Sadly after a few years the owners put the Duck Club up for sale. When it sold, Dads job ended and he got a job at a gas station in Wasco. We then moved to Wasco where I started to high school. Sister Janie, a lady I dearly loved, lived just a few blocks from us. I went to school full-time and as soon as I got out of school, my best friend Peggy and I chopped cotton for her dad. Then, when that was finished I worked at a little restaurant. There was a guy quite a bit older than me that would come into the restaurant. One day he asked me to go out on a date with him. I turned him down. It made him very mad and he asked why I had been so nice to him every time he came to the restaurant. I told him it was my job. He was furious. Several weeks later I was in our house vacuuming. I turned around and there he was standing right behind me with an evil look on his face. I started to run and he took off running after me. He chased me all around our house. I don't know how, but I made it past him and out the front door. I ran down the street to Janie's house. They called the police and put out a restraining order on him. ("But God"!!!) Once again his hand of protection was around me. There were all kinds of weird things that went on. One night my brother went outside to turn off the sprinkler and there was someone, who we believe was him, lying underneath my bedroom window. He took off running and since it was so dark we could not prove it was Bill but we all knew it had to be.

Our church was having a youth revival around that time. Janie told me I could ride to church with her and her boys. For some reason that made Mom so mad and she said I couldn't go. I begged her to let me go, but she would not give in. I wanted to go so badly because I felt like I needed it desperately. I could not stop the tears from flowing. I had fasted for 7 days. So, I begged her to let me go. It made her so mad. She went in the bedroom and got my dad's shotgun, grabbed me by the hair of the head and pulled me down the hallway. She slammed me up against the wall, grabbed that shotgun and told me I better stop crying if I knew what was good for me. About that time my dad came walking in the house. He asked what was going on and when she told him that I wanted to go to church and she didn't want me to, he told her to let me go. ("But God"!!!). It had to have been God that touched my dad's heart that day. I went to church that night and God blessed me unbelievably. God has been so good to me.

Not long after that, my dad met another woman and was having yet another affair. He walked in the house one evening and my mom waylaid him with a frying pan. She put him in the hospital with a concussion. Dad left again and moved in with that lady. He took the car, which was a beautiful red rebel with white leather seats, and left us his junkie old truck. Mom was still working at the City Hall. I was in the girl's athletic association and had various ball practices after school. So, I often walked to Moms place of employment after work. One day my friend Peggy and I caught a ride home with Mom. Mom was very tired and wanted me to drive. While we were pulling out of the parking lot our little red rebel car passed in front of us and Dads mistress was driving it. Mom told me to follow the car. Soon the car stopped at a stop sign and we stopped right behind her. All of a sudden I heard a swishing sound, turned to my right and saw the passenger door open. My mom jumped out of the truck and ran up to the rebel. She opened the passenger door, reached across the seat, grabbed hold of the mistress's hair, pulled her across the seat and on to the sidewalk next to the car. They were on the ground. The mistress fought back and there was screaming, punching, and gouging. Their dresses were above the waist and underwear exposed. Arms and legs were flying. My mom's denture got broken. A huge crowd gathered to see what was going on. I was still sitting at the stop sign, behind the rebel, with my mouth open, when suddenly the rebel began to slowly roll across the 4 lane road in front of us, because there was no one inside the car with their foot on the brake. Then I saw my dad run out of the filling station where he was working. He jumped in the car right before it hit a telephone pole. Someone called the police. They broke up the fight and Mom came back to the truck all bloody and bruised. Since she worked at city hall across the hall from the police station she knew all the police. So no citation was given.

Dad and his mistress moved to Arkansas shortly after the big fight. I didn't see Dad for about 11 years after that.

I graduated from Wasco High with honors. I'm the only one in my family to graduate. I could not have done it without Gods help. I praise him for his goodness.

Our family moved to Delano shortly after I graduated. I went to work for a CPA, McClain and Company. Mr. McClain trained young graduates in bookkeeping and accounting. I was paid $1.65 an hour. Some things Mom said and did, still hurt me deeply but she knew not to raise a hand to me. I continued to live there for my siblings sake and to help out financially. Life seemed to settle down some.

We went on a family vacation to visit family in Arkansas. While we were there, Mom took my siblings by to stay a couple days with Dad and his mistress. When we went to pick them up, my sister Tina said she was staying there. We were devastated. How could we go back to California without her. Mom chased her around the car trying to force her to go with us. But with Dad pulling in one direction and Mom in the other, we drove off without her. I'll never forget that feeling. Within a year Tina was pregnant and came back home to live with us in California. After a few months she had my first niece. What a cutie she was.

We had lots of break ins during this time. We came home from church more than once to find out someone had broke into our home and stole anything of value. Our furniture, including stereos, appliances, silver, guns, even shoes and clothes were gone some times. One time we came home and the back door was standing open. It was obvious thieves had taken most of our stuff. However, it was also obvious they were planning a second trip. Because in the middle of the floor was a pile of small items. Like the toaster oven, toaster, coffee pot, mixer, iron, ironing board, and so on. We came home before they could take the rest of our stuff. It was very scary.("But God"!!!)

One time my aunt went on vacation and asked us to feed her dogs every evening. When we got to her house one day the back door was open. We went in the house and the dogs were going crazy. We very quickly realized there was a robbery taking place, even though we didn't see anyone. My mom immediately called the police and they asked her several questions, then told her to get out of the house immediately, because from what she was telling them the thief was still in the house. So, we ran out of the house and jumped in the car. The police came, but they didn't find anyone. The front door, which was previously closed, was standing open. So, when we ran out the back door and got in the car the thieves probably went out the front door. My uncle had several nice guns in a gun case and things like that. Lots of valuable items were taken. "(But God!!!"). He once again had his hand of protection around us.

I dated some here and there but the only serious relationship was with Brad. We were both out of school, working and in church. We had dated steadily for a couple years. He asked me to marry him and I said yes. Of course we immediately told his parents and my Mom. They were thrilled. By the next day, which was a Sunday, word had already got around. Unfortunately, we did not talk to our pastor before all this. So, on Sunday morning when we went to talk to Pastor he told us he would not marry us. He said we had shown immaturity by not coming to him first, so we needed to wait. He told us we had been exclusive and not dated many others so we needed to take a year and date other people. He told us to play the field and come back in a year. If we still wanted to get married in a year then he would marry us. Back in those days that is how it was. You did not question your pastor. So we obeyed him. Within a year, Brad was engaged to another woman he met from another church. They eloped and moved to the city she was from, a few hours away. My heart was broken. Not long after that, a guy named Wayne came to our church, then a new story begins.

SHATTERED DREAMS

*I*n the winter of 1971 Dessie and Rosie Sexton came to our church. They received the Holy Ghost. Rosie lived in Bakersfield but Dessie lived in Delano where our church was. Not long after they started coming to church, Wayne, who was Rosie's son and Dessie's grandson came to visit them while on leave from the army. He came to church with Dessie and received the Holy Ghost. He stayed with Dessie most of his leave and hung out with our young people's group. That is how we became acquainted. Then each time he was home on leave we got a little closer and eventually started dating.

I only saw his mom, Rosie a few times because she lived in Bakersfield 40 minutes away. She didn't come to church very often. One day, Wayne took me and Dessie to Bakersfield to Rosie's house. Rosie was a very heavy set woman. She was sitting in some man's lap when we walked in. They were making out and everything, right there with other people in the room. I was very uncomfortable and I could not get out of there fast enough. There was people drinking and smoking and just real trashy looking everywhere. We didn't stay very long. I was thankful for that. Wayne's leave was up, so he left the next day.

Several months past and he came home on another leave. He found out his mother had been diagnosed with cancer. We went to see her in the hospital. I think that was the only time he visited her there. It is my understanding that Dessie pretty much raised him because Rosie was unstable. After a few days Wayne left again and supposedly went back to the army base. He was usually gone for a few months before he came back. But, this time he was only gone a few days. When he came back he told everyone that he had received a hardship discharge because he was an only child and his mother was dying. None of us questioned that. We had heard of other similar situations. After that, he never pretended to go back to the army base. He got a job on a farm. We all went on with our lives not ever suspecting anything. He was a very good liar. He was very quiet. He never raised his voice, never really got excited about anything. I look back on it now and think that was the attraction for me. All I had ever known was screaming, hollering and knock down drag outs most every day of my life. So, to be with someone who never raised his voice or showed much emotion of any kind, was a relief. I mistook it for love and caring, when in fact it was lies and deceit. Someone in our church said the quiet ones are the ones you have to look out for. I remember thinking, though, that he would be good to me.

Wayne asked me to marry him and we set the wedding date for December, 1972. Rosie had passed away. Of course we got the OK and all from our pastor before we announced our engagement or anything. I was on cloud nine. Because my Mom had a failed marriage she assumed all marriages failed. When she asked me what made me think mine would last, I told her because I would be such a good wife, he would never have any reason to leave. How little did I know. As the wedding drew near I did all the normal things like putting the engagement in the paper and so on. I had just sent out our wedding invitations when our pastor called me and told me to call off the wedding. I was stunned. I started crying and explained to him that I had already sent out the invitations and the announcement was in the paper. He said he didn't care he wanted me to call it off. He would not tell me the reason why. When I told Wayne, he told me not to worry about it that he would take care of it. The following Sunday, Wayne, went into our pastors office to talk to him and when he came out he said everything was OK and we could be married as planned. When I asked him why Pastor wanted us to call it off, he said it was because the way he had treated his mother while she was in the hospital. You have to remember, in some churches back then, women let the men do all the conversing and counseling. So, we got married as planned. I look back on it now and think how stupid could I be. I should have done everything in my power to find out why Pastor wanted us to call it off, instead of taking Wayne's word for it.

The wedding was beautiful and I thought I was going to have a happy life at last. I just knew our marriage was made in heaven and I would have the life I'd always dreamed of. We stayed in a beautiful hotel at Pismo beach for one night for our honeymoon. When it came time to consummate our marriage, he could not finish his business. I was a virgin and didn't quite know what to expect but I knew that was a little strange. The next morning he acted very weird and then told me he had a cousin who lived close by that he wanted to go see. So, we got dressed, had breakfast and went to his cousins house. It was weird because there was only a blonde haired woman at the house. She and Wayne acted very strange. They left me in a room all alone and went somewhere else in the house for quite some time. Then we left. He evaded all questions I had about the situation. It was just the strangest honeymoon but we finally consummated our marriage and began our married life. I was so happy for about three months. Then my world came crumbling down.

Three months into our marriage I was at work when two men in black suits came into my office, flashed their badges and said "We are with the FBI. We have your husband in custody. He is absent without leave from the army, and has been for over a year. I could not believe what I was hearing. So that meant, Wayne was AWOL almost the entire time we were dating. I have so many questions. Where did he go when he would tell us his leave was over and he had to go back to the army base? I freaked out. I broke down. They led me to the police car so I could tell Wayne goodbye. I begged them to let me go to jail with him. They put him in jail first and then he was transferred to the army prison. I did not know how I was going to make it without him. It felt like part of me was gone.

I had to move out of the little apartment we lived in to make ends meet. My brother Mike and some men from the church moved me while I was at work. When they did, they found dirty magazines under the big braided rug I had in our living room. One of the elderly men told me that night and said we needed to let Pastor know, but he would leave that up to me. I was stunned. He said the magazines were the worst of the worst and absolutely gross. That was all I needed on top of everything else.

I moved into a little cottage behind some people who went to our church. I left the bookkeeping job and went to work for the bank, making more money. I got very sick on my first day of employment at the bank. I went to the doctor and found out I was pregnant with my oldest daughter Shanna. I was thrilled. The sad thing was, while he was in the army brig, right after I found out I was pregnant, someone from his past told me he had a wife and baby in Vietnam. They said they thought he was still in love with her and missed her and the baby so much that he wasn't thinking straight and that's why he went AWOL. I later tried to talk to him about it. He said he married her but it wasn't legal and there was no proof the baby was his because the Vietnamese slept with lots of men. He told me not to worry about it. I remember thinking I wish someone had told me this before we married.

I wrote the congressman of California, Bob Mathias, a letter asking him to release Wayne from prison. I explained about his mom dying and me being pregnant. Amazingly, Bob Mathias, wrote me back and said he would do everything in his power to get Wayne out. About three weeks after that, I got the call that the army was releasing him with a dishonorable discharge. My mom, Dessie and I drove down to get him. It was so strange, because he didn't act at all remorseful. He actually acted like he was embarrassed for us to be there. He did apologize to the church, asked for forgiveness and prayed through. Once we got home he seemed to adapt and as time went on I thought we actually had a really good and happy marriage.

Our daughter, Shanna was born on our first anniversary, December, 1973. I cannot explain the joy. I had never known that kind of love until my baby girl. I truly thought I could never love anything as much as I did her. She was the happiest baby and quite the show off. She was beautiful. Back then the men had to wait in the waiting room, during child birth. As soon as they took me to my room and Shanna to the nursery Wayne left. We were in the hospital 3 days. I hardly saw Wayne the entire three days. I didn't think much about it but wanted to see him. My sister Jackie bought the cutest little balloon lamp and brought it to the hospital. I was upset because I hadn't seen Wayne. She said, " don't worry, he borrowed some money from me, so I'm sure he's buying you flowers or something, and will be in soon." He never did either. He took Dessie out for lunch with the money he had borrowed from Jackie. I was very sick and almost passed out more than once during the hospital stay. I had to have a transfusion because I have 0 positive Rh negative blood and Shanna was another blood type. We were finally released from the hospital. Wayne picked me up from the hospital and took us straight to his grandmother's house for a few days. We slept on a foldout sofa with Shanna in the bassinet next to me. The next day I was in severe pain and told him I needed some of the items the hospital had prescribed when I left, feminine pads, tucks and so on. He got mad and said we didn't have the money. My mom and sisters came to see us and could see I had been crying. They wound up going to the drugstore and buying the things I needed. ("But God"!!!) He's always an on time God.

The next week we went home and started our lives as three. I was in heaven. I quit my job at the bank and took a babysitting job so I could stay home with Shanna. I was so happy. Everyone thought we had a marriage made in heaven, including me. My sister once said she hoped, when she got married that she and her husband was as happy as Wayne and I were.

When Shanna was about six months old I told Wayne we were out of everything to eat and ask him if he would mind running to the corner store and get us some milk, orange juice and eggs before he went to work. We only had one car. I just got paid so I gave him all the money. He went to the store and came back with the items I requested. He didn't offer to give back the change and I didn't think anything about it. He kissed me bye, went to work, told his boss he was quitting, picked up his check, walked to the freeway and hitch hiked out of state. By 6 o'clock that night I knew something was wrong. I called his boss and he told me Wayne came in about 10 o'clock, picked up his check and quit. I was devastated. My whole world came crashing down. I thought I was going to die. His boss said he left the car and had another check coming the following week and that he had tried to get it but they wouldn't give it to him. I could not believe Wayne took the change from my weekly income and also tried to get the next check he had coming, knowing that the few items I had ask him to get was all Shanna and I had. His boss told me they could not legally give me the check but if I would come out there the next week they would pull some strings and see what they could do to get me that check. I went the next week and sat in the office forever, holding Shanna and just crying. I could do nothing for days but cry. Shanna was the only thing in the world I had and I was the only thing in the world she had. It took a lot of red tape but they finally let me have that check and our car. ("But God"!!!) He is our provider!

I was able to get groceries for a couple weeks, put gas in the car to tide us over while looking for a job. I put in applications all over town. But there were no openings anywhere at that time. I took the only thing available. It was chopping cotton from 4 AM until 4 PM each day. I was so devastated and could barely function. I would get up about 3:30 AM each day, take Shanna to Dessie's and drive to the cotton field. I couldn't eat because I was so upset. I dropped 15 pounds in two weeks. One day I passed out right there in the field. From that point on everyone working with me made me eat. They all brought extra food and nearly forced it down me. Some others from the church worked with me. They were a great help. So, I began to heal. Then, about 2 1/2 months later Wayne called, out of the blue, and told me he was in another state and wanted us to come there. I went the next day and talked with my pastor. He told me to not go. He said I had no idea what Wayne was mixed up in or for sure where he was or what he was doing. He said he was afraid I would get there and be in a big mess. He feared for mine and Shanna's life. He told me to tell Wayne if he really wanted to be together he had to come back, pray through and prove himself. Pastor told me not to take him back immediately, to make him prove himself before letting him back in our home. A few weeks later Wayne came back. He supposedly prayed through. Unfortunately, I didn't listen to my pastor and after two or three weeks I took him back with open arms. I just wanted so desperately to have our family back together. I prayed everything would be OK. He did apologize to the church again and ask the church and me for forgiveness. I guess I am the dumbest person in the world because I really believed everything would be fine. I am the world's biggest optimist. It seems like whatever happens in my life, I may be down for a while, but when it passes, I believe everything is going to be OK.

Wayne wasn't home very long when weird stuff started happening. Shanna got the chickenpox, so we decided to take turns going to church. One of us would go to church and the other stay home with her. Then the next church service we would switch. He said he was really tired and wanted to stay home the first night. Some friends picked me up for church. In the middle of church I went out to the church phone and called the house to see how Shanna was doing. I didn't get an answer and just had a very weird feeling. So, my friend told me to take their car and go home and check on everything. When I drove up to our house Wayne was sitting in our car with Shanna. She was standing up in the front seat beside him. I could tell she had been crying. She had one of my long dresses wrapped around her, but nothing else. She was totally naked, no diaper or anything. When I ask him what he was doing he said Shanna wanted an ice cream, so he took her to TG&Y. It was freezing outside, people had to go inside of TG&Y to get an ice cream. Shanna was totally naked, running fever and had chicken pox. That just did not make any sense to me. He couldn't explain the dress, he couldn't explain why she was totally naked, why he took her out in freezing cold weather with the chickenpox or what they were doing sitting in the car. Bizarre! It scared me.

About a month later he said he was sick and didn't feel like going to church. So, Shanna and I went. When I got home from church the front door and screen door was standing open. As I drove up the driveway I could see that our furniture was overturned and there was total chaos in the house. I sat in the car not knowing what to do. I was too scared to get out. About that time Wayne came walking from around the outside corner of our house along the street. He was a mess. I could tell he'd been in a fight. When I ask him what was going on he said he fell asleep and someone came in the house. He said he woke up and surprised them. But, the cushions were all off the furniture, the tables were overturned, the drawers pulled out, and all kinds of stuff that pointed to the fact that who-ever was in that house was looking for something. A few days later he bought a really mean dog and kept him tied right by the front door. We had the dog just a few days and someone drove up in a car and stole him. Right after that Wayne kissed me by with the pretense of going to work and left for the second and last time. I believe he was mixed up with drugs, mafia, Mexican cartel or something, because there are several other situations that would take too long to describe. After he left, I found out he was involved with another woman and possibly had another family altogether. So, my pastor told me to divorce him because this was obviously going to be a pattern. I think Pastor knew some things that I didn't. I was so lonely and hurt.("But God"!!!) He is our comforter.

Being a divorcée is a lonely life. None of my married friends wanted to hang out because they didn't want a single woman around their husband. On the other hand my single friends didn't want me around because I had a baby. One time a single friend invited me to ride with a group to a fellowship meeting. I was so excited to be going somewhere. Shanna was very well behaved and I had no one to leave her with. Everyone knew that. When I arrived at my friend's house, she walked out to my car and told me I was no longer invited if I was bringing Shanna. I realized then, that none of them had a clue what I was going through. The hurt was almost more than I could bare. ("But God"!!!) He wrapped his loving arms around me and wiped away each tear.

Life went on. I got a job at JC Penny. A sweet family in our church babysat Shanna. I hated leaving my baby each day and couldn't wait to pick her up. She was my light in a dark world.

We were at a family gathering several years later when suddenly, out of the blue, Wayne drove up. Where did he come from? Where had he been all this time? He motioned for me to come to the car. We talked for a couple minutes. I picked Shanna up so he could see her. He held her for a minute. He evaded any questions I asked and would not divulge any information. Then he left and we never saw him again.

DECEIVED

*A*s the months passed by, a young man by the name of Bill visited our church. He said he had just moved to Bakersfield from Hobbs, NM. As time went on, it seemed like everyone I knew told me God sent Bill there for me and Shanna. People started pushing us together. For instance, suddenly my married friends started coming around again and would invite me to go eat with them after church. Then when Shanna and I got to the restaurant they we're all seated to where the only spot available, at the half circle table, was next to Bill. I would attempt to sit at another table and they would tell me there was plenty of room and asked me to please sit with them. The older women that were my mentors would tell me it was God ordained. Unfortunately, I believed them. It wasn't long before we became interested in each other.

Bills dad and stepmother (The Helms) lived in Hobbs, NM. They owned a large roofing company there. His Dad had a heart attack. So, he called Bill and asked him to move back there and help with the company. Bill told his parents that we were dating and he wanted to marry me. They told him to ask us to come with him. They said they would help me find a job and Shanna and I could live with them as long as we wanted. My parents, siblings and entire family had moved to Alaska to work on the pipeline and supposedly make a lot of money. I had nothing to keep me in Delano. Bill asked me to marry him. So, after much prayer I said yes and decided to step out by faith and go with him. Since we were not married yet, we wanted to keep everything above board. So, we did not travel by car. We got tickets to ride a bus so we would be in public the entire time and not be spending the night together, and so on.

I let my family know where we were going and sent them phone numbers and the Helms address in case they needed to reach me. We hadn't been there very long when my mom called me and told me she laid awake at night thinking about the needless beatings she gave me. I knew that was her way of saying she was sorry. My heart went out to her. She made things right with God and me. She lived for him to the best of her ability. I'm so thankful for that.

When we got to the Helms they welcomed me and Shanna with open arms. They immediately fell in love with Shanna and I was so happy, because they treated her like a grandchild they had known forever. They were so kind to me. I truly felt loved. Bill went to work for his Dad at Helms Roofing Company and I got a job at First National Bank. Shanna and I had a room next to Mom and Dad Helms and Bill stayed in a little add on room at the end of the house. He made me think he was so holy. Many nights we would pray together in the living room after everyone had gone to bed. After a few months we got married. We had a sweet little wedding with family members.

It wasn't long until we got our own cute little place in town. Bills grandma, on his dad's side, lived down the street from us and kept Shanna while I was at work. Shanna seemed to really like her and vice versa. She gave Shanna a little sock monkey and that became her favorite toy. We found a wonderful church there, but several months later I began to notice a change in Bill. He made excuses why he couldn't make it to church. He started hanging out with some cousins that were into drugs, alcohol and not very nice things. Little by little the world began to draw him. He started drinking, smoking, and hanging out with them more and more. He told me he never was really in church. He said he only pretended to be a Christian just so he could get me.

The Helms decided to retire and move to their ranch in Oklahoma. Because of Bills track record they did not ask him to run the business. So, it wasn't long before Bill was without a job. I could not get him to work. I became pregnant with Kerri. I had complications and was deathly sick my first trimester, so unfortunately I was unable to continue working at the bank. Bill refused to get another job and told me to go to welfare and ask for help. Shanna and I walked across town to the Welfare department to apply for food stamps. I don't recall the reason, but I was turned down. We were just about out of food, necessities, and everything. There were a couple weeks we lived off potatoes that someone had put on our front porch. I started feeling better and was out of the danger zone by my 4th month carrying Kerri. So, I put on a top big enough to hide my pregnancy and walked to Dunlap's Department Store to apply for a job. I thought I fooled them, but later my boss told me she knew I was pregnant, but felt so sorry for me that she gave me the job anyway. It was winter time. The only shoes I had was sandals. So, I walked to work every day, in the snow, wearing sandals. I cannot begin to describe how cold my toes got.

I left Shanna with Bill while I worked, since he was not working, never thinking of anything amiss. Our electricity had been turned off and we lived using a coil oil lamp at night. One day I came home from work, Shanna was sitting on the braided rug on the floor. I picked her up and was loving on her and holding her in my lap when Bill started laughing. I asked what was so funny and he said "watch this". He snapped his fingers at her, pointed to the (blank) TV and said, in a mean, raised voice, "watch that TV." With a terrified look she quickly turned her head around and stared at that blank TV. I was mortified and began to cry. I wondered what other mean things he was doing to her. My heart was broken for my baby girl. Bill said he was just being funny and would never hurt her. I was so upset. I put Shanna in the stroller, went to the nearest pay phone and called my friends in California to come and get us. All Bill did was drink, smoke, have parties with his cousins and sleep. Come to find out he was an alcoholic before he was saved. He was treading on dangerous ground by going back to that, after God had delivered him. Life was horrible and with the Helms gone I knew I didn't want to give birth to Kerri there. So, I was ready to go home to California. When our friends got to our house a couple days later, we were getting in the car and Bill jumped in with us. He promised he would get back in church, straighten up his life and never treat Shanna like that again. So, we moved back to California. I never left her alone with him again. I watched things carefully and never saw him be mean or hateful to her again. She never again acted afraid of him and they seemed fine.

Everything seemed to go well the first few months back in California. We lived with Bills real mom and stepdad, Joyce and Ernie, until we got jobs and were on our feet. I had never met them. They were so sweet to Shanna and I thought all was well. Bill was working in the oilfield. I was so big with Kerri by then, I couldn't get a job. One day I got in our car and found a pair of earrings. When I asked Bill whose they were he said he didn't know. I was about 7 months pregnant with Kerri at the time. One night right in the middle of intimacy he rolled off and said "I cannot do this. I want you and Shanna to pack your bags and leave in the morning. Call your mom and have her come get you". I was stunned and did not know what I was going to do. I had no place to go. I definitely was not going to call my mom. So, the next morning I got up and just pretended like everything was fine. I don't know what happened but he never mentioned it again. My intention was to stay until Kerri was born and then find a job and an apartment for me, Shanna and Kerri. But once Kerri was born it was like a light switch came on and Bill tried to step it up and be a good husband and dad for a while. He still drank and so on but seemed to settle down.

Right before Kerri was born we got our own little apartment. Bill went to work at a service/ gas station. The owner was a sweet lady named Lyda, who took us under her wing. She tried to get Bill off alcohol. Bill became manager of the service station. He worked the evening shift.

Kerri was born in April, 1976 and things were good. I realized at that moment that a Mother can love one child as much as the other. What joy she was. She was a little spit fire. Oh how she loved her big sister Shanna. People always commented on how well they played together.

We lived in a little house where you had to drive down an ally to get to. It was ok, but a little scary sometimes. One night I went to buy groceries and when I came home there were police helicopters above our house. When I pulled in our driveway, I was approached by police officers and told to stay in my car until they made sure our home was safe to enter. Also, they searched my car and looked in the trunk to make sure the fugitive they were looking for was not there. They ask me numerous questions to rule out I was not providing a getaway for the perpetrator. Once they were satisfied, they helped me and my girls into our house and made sure we were locked up tight. For all we knew the perpetrator was hiding somewhere watching everything that was going on. (" BUT GOD"!!!) His hand of protection was on us. That was so scary. I started looking for a new place to live.

Since Bill worked evenings I did most of the daily chores in the evening. Buying groceries, going to the laundromat and so on were done at night, so me and the girls could spend time with him during the day. There was a laundromat across the street from where he worked. So, for safety, I always went there to do laundry. One evening, as I was putting the girls and laundry in the car a man approached me and ask if I needed help. I told him no and thanked him for asking. However, he just started putting my laundry baskets into my car. I had already put the girls in. I thanked him, opened my door and got in. To my surprise, when I got in the car he was sitting in the passenger seat. He then began to say some very vulgar and explicit things that he was going to do to me. I was scared to death. I was praying profusely. I was calling on the name of Jesus. I told him my husband worked at the station across the street and he was watching us. I told him that was the reason I came to that particular Laundromat only. I could tell the man didn't know if he should believe me or not. He said a few curse words and made some explicit gestures but, thank God he opened the door and walked away. ("But God!!!") He protected me once again. I immediately locked the doors. I was shaking like a leaf and immediately drove across the street to the station. It was reported but nothing ever came of it. I look back on it now and I know that man had some evil plans. I know God rescued me. Oh, I am so thankful for his protecting hand.

Once I got my strength back from Kerri's birth, I went to work for American National Bank. I was able to find a precious daycare for the girls. I hated leaving them every day but knowing they were well taken care of made it easier. Shortly after I started working at the bank, Bill quit his job at the station and went to work as an insurance salesman. Eventually we moved into a beautiful three bedroom two bath brick home. All seemed well. However, he could not stop drinking, and things began to go downhill fast. He began missing days at work. His boss would call me and asked me if I knew where he was, which I didn't. I finally told him if his boss called me one more time, I was going to quit my job so that he would be forced to go to work. So, after months and months of calls from his boss and fight's because he wouldn't work, I turned in my notice at the bank and started an in home daycare, thinking it would force him to go to work.

Our life became a constant turmoil of him being drunk, staying out all hours of the night in bars, strip clubs and so on.

One day some friends of mine, Donna and Delilah, brought their kids and came to visit from Delano, which was a city about 30 miles from where we lived. That was during the time self serve gas pumps were invented. Delilah did not know how to use them so she asked Bill if he would go with her to pump the gas. That was around 6 PM. By 2 AM the next morning they still had not come back. Donna had to call her husband to come and get her, their kids, and Delilah's kids. Bill and Delilah drove into our driveway some time before dawn. As he came staggering into the house, I hollered at Delilah and ask her how it felt to be like Connie. You see, several years before this, Delilah's husband had an affair with my cousin Connie. Delilah didn't say anything. She just drove off. However, Bill suddenly looked like the devil himself and charged at me. I took off running. I ran through the house into the bathroom and locked the door. He proceeded to kick the door down. The door fell on me but I was able to climb over it, get around Bill and run into the bedroom. Bill was right behind me. I jumped on the bed and covered my head with my arms to soften the blows he was giving. He was on top of me throwing punches as hard as he could. Then he suddenly passed out on the bed. I slowly got up and made my way into the kitchen to clean myself up and then to the living room where I laid on the sofa. I had a huge knot on the side of my head right by my temple. I was so thankful I had put the girls to sleep with the fan running, or it would have scared them to death. ("BUT GOD"!!!) He protected them from that and protected me from being beaten to death. I truly believe God caused Bill to pass out during the beating. While I lay there on the sofa crying, there was a knock at the door. It was Delilah asking if she could come in and apologize for her actions. I opened the door and when she saw my face she began to cry and apologize. She said she thought we should call the hospital to see if I should go and be checked out. I told her to just call the hospital and tell them that her daughter fell against the door knob and had a huge knot by her temple and ask them if it was dangerous. So, she did just that. The operator on the other end of the phone line asked her several questions like "how old is your daughter. Delilah said "I don't know let me ask her." The operator said "you don't know how old your daughter is?" LOL! Delilah got so flustered she told them her daughter was 27 years old. The operator ask, "your daughter is 27 years old and she hit her head on a doorknob?" By the time she was off the phone I was dying laughing because everything she told them made no sense. Once Delilah was convinced I was ok, she went home.

I had determined I was leaving the next day. I told Bill that I would put up with a lot of things, all his drinking and carousing and all. But, I had determined in my heart, I would never be beat again, once I was out of my childhood home. The next day was Kerri's 3rd birthday though. I had planned a party for that day. I planned to leave as soon as the party was over. The Helms called to wish her happy birthday, then they asked to talk with Bill. Not knowing that he had started drinking again, they told him they had moved back to Hobbs, took the company back over and desperately needed us to move back there to help them in the business. They did not know what had been going on in our home and thought everything was fine. They promised us a lot of good things, including putting a down payment on a house for us. Bill hung up the phone and begged me to move back to Hobbs with him. He said he would get back in church. He promised everything would be great. I could not stand the thought of another divorce. So, with new hopes and dreams, we rented a U-Haul truck packed up our stuff, said our good-byes to friends and family and moved back to Hobbs to help the Helms again. If Bill would have played his cards right, done what he was supposed to do and stayed out of trouble he could have become a wealthy man and owner of the roofing company. The little house they put a down payment on was ready for us to move into when we got there. It was a cute little two bedroom.

I started daycare in the home and he started to work as foreman of the roofing company. Everything seemed to be going well until Bill started coming home wearing new, expensive boots and other expensive items that I knew had not come out of his paycheck. When I asked him how he got them he always said they were a gift from clients. It wasn't long until the Helms found out he was stealing from the company. He embezzled quite a bit of money. We also found out he and the roofing crew he was in charge of, while working out of town, were not only working, but they were also having orgies in the hotel rooms and all kinds of evil. Someone took pictures to prove it.

Mom Helms told me that Bill sat in her office, with tears running down his face and told her he knew that me, the girls and that job were the best things that ever happened to him, but the world had too much of a hold on him and he could not help himself. The Helms fired him. He had a girlfriend by the name of Beverly. I found out about them and learned that's where he spent much of his time, instead of working. I had reached my limit and told him I was done and could not live like that anymore. He was furious. It wasn't long until he left Hobbs with his girlfriend Beverly and moved back to Bakersfield, California.

I went on with life there in Hobbs. One day I took all my daycare kids to the mall to see Santa. When we got back to my house Bill was standing on my front porch holding an ax. He was so mad that I had gone on with my life. I had left him several times in the past and always took him back, because he made promises that he did not keep. I could not take the infidelity and abuse any longer. He had gone in my house and chopped up everything, my piano, my dishwasher, washing machine and so on. I was scared to death but I got in his face and told him that the Helms had talked me into filing a restraining order and that I had every police protection number at the touch of a button and they would have him before he got to the edge of town. He knew the Helms had great pull with everyone in Hobbs and he knew I was telling the truth. I was shaking like a leaf. Seeing him with that ax was so frightening. He got in his car and left. That was the last time I saw him. He went back to California and continued to live with his girlfriend Beverly. They later separated. Sometime later I applied for child support from him. The social worker told me he was a bad alcoholic and mentally unstable. She said he called himself the terminator and if we ever approached him again he would kill me and Kerri. The social worker said he was very scary and for our safety I should just leave it alone.

After Bill was gone, a family member told me that a few years before we married, Bill was arrested and spent time in prison for armed robbery. That was so scary. I realized I had spent 4 years with a man I didn't even know. ("But God"!!!) I'm so thankful he kept his loving arms of protection around Me, Shanna and Kerri. The bible warns us of wolves in sheep clothing.

MIRACLES

I mentioned in the latter part of the first chapter of this book that Brad and I used to date. Many years ago Brad asked me to marry him but our pastor would not marry us and told us to play the field for a year. Brad wound up marrying someone else and so did I.

Years later Brad ran into some mutual friends of ours. He had been divorced for several years. When he heard about Bill and my failed marriage, he called me. I was not interested in another relationship. However, it wasn't long before he moved to Hobbs, rented a house across the street from us and began to pursue me. He paid me to do his laundry. Eventually we began to date. He asked me to marry him but I told him no. I just could not go through the hurt and pain again should something happen to our marriage. He waited a few months then came to my house with a calendar in hand. He sat down, opened the calendar to June 6, 1980, and said "this is what we're going to do. We're going to get married June 6. Shanna and Kerri will spend the night with the Helms while we honeymoon overnight. The next day we will pick Shanna and Kerri up and drive to California where we will get my three kids (from his previous marriage) and bring them home for the summer." So, that is exactly what we did. Mom and Dad Helms fell in love with Brad and helped us in every way they could. They were so happy when I said yes. Because they knew how Bill had treated me. They had disowned him but, they still called me daughter and we remained close the rest of their lives. When Brad and I married, Dad Helms walked me down the aisle and gave me away to Brad. The girls stayed the night with the Helms while we honeymooned. The next morning we picked the girls up and headed to California. We had an enjoyable trip there. When we picked up his three kids, Denita, Darren and Duane their mother had put all their clothes in a laundry basket. There were roaches running everywhere. We drove out to an open field and took each article of clothing, shook it out and made sure we got rid of all the roaches. Then we headed back home to Hobbs. As we were driving through Blithe, California our vehicle broke down. We found a mechanics shop. Thankfully there was a hotel across the street. Once we were settled in the hotel and had our vehicle in the shop we walked across the street to Dairy Queen. When we walked in with five kids, we were asked if they were all ours. Brad said "yes, and we just got married last week." They all got a big laugh. I could feel my face turning red. As we visited with the staff we told our story. When it came time to pay the bill they told us the meal was paid for. A wedding gift to us from them and wished us the best of luck. I will never forget that act of kindness. Everything was so new and scary. From the beginning of our marriage we drove to California every summer and brought Brads kids from his previous marriage home with us for the summer. We always tried to include some fun things, like trips to Disneyland and so forth. I grew to love Denita, Darin and Duane and they loved me. They were so hungry for attention and love and we tried to give them that.

I was so thankful and blessed that Brad took my girls as his own. When their biological Fathers left they never had anything to do with them. Brad loved them and they loved him. He has been a great Dad to them.

The Pastor of the UPC church that I had attended since I first moved to Hobbs, married Brad and me. So, we continued to go there. I played the piano and taught Sunday School. One Sunday there was a tremendous thunderstorm during church service. We could hear the rain pounding on the roof but did not realize there was flooding. We waded in ankle deep water to get to our car. We drove a couple blocks, when suddenly we were in about 4ft of water. We had no control of our car. It was floating like a boat and bumping into other cars and other cars were bumping into us, telephone poles, trees and other things. Water began to rush inside the car. The girls were frightened and screaming. Brad and I rolled our windows down and crawled out into the freezing water. He grabbed Shanna and pulled her out the window while I grabbed Kerri. We trudged through the swiftly moving water, carrying the girls, with torrential rains coming down, until we reached higher ground and made it back to the church parsonage, where our Pastor and wife supplied us with dry robes used for baptisms. They took us home once the storm passed and the water receded. That was so scary. ("But God"!!!) Once again he put a hedge of protection around us. Our car was pretty much totaled.

In 1982 a new family started coming to our church, by the name of Overman. They quickly became our best friends. Our Son, Marlin Douglas, was born July of that year. Oh what joy! We were having a boy! God knew what he was doing when he gave us Marley. Brad wanted to name him after his dad and his best friend and that's what we did. Marley has brought so much joy and laughter into our lives. I loved this little tiny human just as much as I did the other two God had given me. Marley was a miracle. I started having complications one month before he was born. Then, I woke up one morning and was hemorrhaging. Consequently I was hospitalized and even though I was in labor, it was not progressing. So, after many hours of labor I was given aggressive medication to speed things up. After a few hours a nurse came to check on me and frantically went running out of the room, then came back with another nurse. They told me my baby was in distress, so they had called the doctor and was taking me straight to delivery. As Marley was being born and his head was out, the doctor looked at me and said "do not push when the next contraction comes, or you will kill your baby, because the chord is wrapped around his neck three times. As I laid there holding back the natural urge to push that comes with each delivery contraction, the pain was almost more than I could bare. But, I watched as the doctor carefully slid that chord over our sons head, one, two, three times. Then he said "now you can push." In those days they didn't have the technology to determine if it was a boy or girl, ahead of time. The very moment I saw my baby was a boy, and he was going to be ok, I began to rejoice. The tears were flowing and I loudly thanked God. I think I embarrassed the medical team as I praised the Lord. ("But God!!!")

The Overman's were such a great source of help and we learned so much from them. Not long after Marley was born they were transferred to Levelland, Texas. They loved it there and wanted us to move there. We found a nice home right across the street from them. So, in November of 1982 we packed our station wagon and trailer to start our new life in Texas.

When we pulled in front of our new home, there was a crowd of people from the church waiting to move us in. By midnight that night every room of furniture was set up in our home, every pot and pan, dish and glass was in the cabinets. Every linen was in the linen closet. What a blessing that was.

So, our life in Texas began. I was happier than I'd ever been. Brad worked at a hardware store and I had an in home daycare. It wasn't long before I was playing the piano for the church, Brad was leading song service, we were over the Sunday School department and every part of our life was working for the Lord. We were very busy, I loved every minute. We started a bus ministry, but because we didn't have buses we brought children in our station wagon and other cars. Our Sunday School Evangelism Team was bringing about 60 kids to church every Sunday. We had a program or two and the parents started coming. We were having a great revival. Our church was like one big family. My daycare was thriving. Brad was doing well on his job. The kids were doing well in school. I was very happy. Then, a couple years later, a spirit of adultery moved into our church.

A man in our church called me and told me he was in love with me. Then he asked me if I felt the same. I told him no. I reminded him of how wonderful his beautiful wife and family was. He asked me to pray for him. He then made things right with his wife and they are still happily married. Not long after that, I noticed something was bothering Brad. When I asked him what was wrong he told me that one of my BEST friends had been visiting him, every day at the western store he worked at. She had expressed her desire for them to run off together. She told him she was in love with him. She was relentless and was determined they would be together. She was willing to leave her husband and two children. I won't go into any more detail here. But, if the devil had his way, I would have lost my husband. ("But God!!!")

I told him I was serving him and the devil notice. I said "HE IS NOT GETTING YOU". I admit I was talking about the devil and that woman. I cannot begin to describe the hurt and pain I felt. My heart broke.

Our Pastor had a conversation with the lady and told her she needed to apologize to me. She came to my house but all she said was "I never meant for it to go this far." She was very plain and didn't know how to fix her hair or anything. So, for quite some time she had been coming to our house, every Thursday night for me to fix her hair and, unknown to me, see Brad. She had the nerve to ask me if I was going to continue doing her hair. When I said no, she wanted to know why. I told her, because all this time I didn't know I had been making her pretty for (MY) husband.

Our Pastor told her to stay out of the Cowboy store Brad worked at and never go back. A couple months after that, Brad called me one day and told me he wanted to be upfront with everything, so he needed to tell me that she came in the store. I was fuming mad. I called Pastor and told him to tell her to keep her rear out of that store. He said he would. However, at that moment he told me he was seeing hate build up in me. He said they have asked forgiveness and prayed through and going on with life. If the trumpet sounded they would probably make it. But, would I? When he asked me that, I thought "I have every right to hate her." But, my heart was pricked and I fell to the floor as soon as we hung up, and repented. However, the deep hurt and pain held on. It just seemed I could not move forward.

At the first of the year we had communion and foot washing at our church. The women were in one room and the men in another. For foot washing we had water in a square Rubbermaid tub. It was placed on the floor between two chairs. A woman would sit in a chair while another woman would kneel down in front of her and wash her feet. Then they would switch. The woman whose feet had just been washed would then wash someone's feet.

While each person was washing feet or getting their feet washed the rest of the ladies made a circle around them and prayed for them. The presence of the Lord moved into that place and chains were broken. When the woman who had been chasing Brad sat down in the chair to have her feet washed, I immediately felt a hand on my back pushing me forward to wash her feet. To this day I do not know if it was the hand of God I felt or someone in the crowd. Because I certainly didn't go there intending to wash her feet. However, as I knelt there washing her feet, I could feel God washing me. Every bit of hurt, pain, and suffering was washed away. It was like a warm shower flowing over me. I was lost in the spirit. When I finished, she got up, we hugged and she walked away. I sat down and someone else washed my feet. I praised God for taking all that bitterness away. After that night, I was able to move forward and began to heal. He helps us through our darkest nights and makes all things new. We are a testimony that marriages can be mended and God can do great things through what the devil tried to destroy. We recently celebrated our 42nd anniversary. No, everything has not been perfect and we've had many test and trials. But, all and all

God has been so good. He has given us the most beautiful, wonderful family. We are blessed.

During the healing process the Brumley family moved to Levelland, from Houston area and started coming to our church. I introduced myself to them and welcomed them. I was still numb from all that had just happened in my life. So, I don't know if it was my countenance or what but within a few days Sandy Brumley somehow got my phone number and called me. She said "I know you don't think I know what you're going through but, I do, and I just want you to know I'm praying for you." As tears were flowing down my face I thought, how could you possibly know? You don't even know me." I politely thanked her and hung up. As we became friends later, I found out she really did know. Her husband Jimmy Brumley had a background in music and soon became our music director at church. Sandy was involved in SS ministry and started helping us in that department, among other things. They had three kids, Jimbo and Emily were twins and Josh was the youngest. The twins were about a year older than our son Marley and Josh was the same age as him. It wasn't long before the Brumley's invited us over for supper. I was so surprised when the supper consisted of frozen pizza, salad and ice cream for dessert. It was so simple. No muss no fuss. It was the best dinner we had ever had at a friend's house. I always thought I had to cook an extravagant meal and spotless my house for company. Then by the time company arrived I was so tired I couldn't enjoy it. That night I learned I didn't have to do all that. The Brumley's quickly became our best friends. Brad and Jimmy really hit it off. Sandy and I could just be ourselves around each other and the kids all enjoyed time together. Shanna and Kerri became their traveling babysitters and enjoyed traveling to and from Houston with them. Marley, Josh, Jimbo and Emily were inseparable.

Not long after Marley started school I closed my daycare and started working at American National bank part time and Walmart part time. Then eventually went to work full time at the bank. It was a busy but good life. Sometimes when things became too hectic and I could see my kids getting way too tired, we would all just take a day off from school and work. We stayed in our pajamas all day, ordered pizza or something out and watched movies, read books, played games or whatever, to just unwind. We did this especially when we had two or three week revival. I preferred them missing school over missing church. I also didn't want them to be too tired at church to receive what God had for them.

God performed so many miracles when we were in Levelland. At one point every tire on our car needed replaced. We did not have the money to buy a set of new tires. So, we carried an air compressor tank in our car. We didn't tell anyone, but one day after Sunday School all our tires were flat in front of the church. So someone saw Brad pull the air compressor out of the car and air up all the tires. A few days later we heard a commotion outside our house and when we looked out the window we saw a tire company taking off the old tires and putting new ones on. We asked them what was going on. They informed us that someone, who wanted to remain anonymous, ordered the tires and paid for them to be delivered to our address. What a blessing that was. We never found out who did that but we thank God for them to this day. ("BUT GOD"!!!) He will supply our every need.

Another miracle was when Brad got appendicitis and had to have his appendix removed. The surgery was performed and he healed well. Later we found out the doctor who performed the surgery was a fake. He didn't even have a license to practice medicine. ("BUT GOD"!!!) He guided the surgeons hands and protected Brad.

God also healed me. I had not been feeling well. I went to the doctor. They ran blood work. Test came back positive for lupus. I asked the doctor if it was fatal and she said there was normally about a ten year life span with the type I had. I was so scared. My girls were early teens, and our Son about 7. I was so worried about what would happen to them. I prayed, did research and begged God for healing. To say I was distraught is an understatement. Not long after the diagnoses, we went to a Carmen concert with the Brumleys. God moved in that concert. Carmen told everyone to reach over, lay hands on someone and pray for them. I don't know who all prayed for me, but God healed me that night. I felt his healing power. ("BUT GOD"!!!) His healing virtue flowed through me.

Another miracle was when God gave us one of our children back from Satan's clutches. We had a blended family, his, mine and ours. Although Brad's kids from a previous marriage lived with their mom most of the time, they lived with us for a period of time and one of them lived with us a lot longer. One of the worst moments of my life was when one of our 6 children who only had 4 months before their high school graduation, got mixed up with the wrong crowd and told us they were leaving home, quitting school and going to live with a family who was known to have problems in several scandalous situations. I cried, prayed and begged them not to go. I even talked with the police. However, since they were 17 years old there was nothing I could do but pray. I balled my eyes out as they walked out with suitcases in hand. As they stood in the hallway waiting for their ride, with tears running down my face, I told them that I had no idea where this path would lead. I let them know that even though they may go to the very depths of hell and back, when they were ready to come home, we would be waiting with open arms. I tried to get them to understand they had no idea what was out there in the world. With tears in their eyes they looked at me and said " Mom, I know what you are telling me is probably true. But, I've got to find out for myself." I knew then that no amount of talking or begging was going to change their mind. At that moment I told her the same thing I told my husband many years ago. I said, "Well, I am serving you and the devil notice right now, HE IS NOT GETTING YOU!!!" After they left I went in their room and told God I knew none of their belongings were in there but I was pleading the blood over them. I laid hands on the walls, on the curtains, on anything that was left behind. Then I fell down on the floor and interceded. God's love washed over me. Later that evening I told our son Marley, to get his bible quiz book and quiz cards so we could go over his quizzing. I was so weary from the day's events. As I sat in the chair listening to Marley quote scripture one of his scriptures was Ps. 32:7. "Thou art my hiding place; thou shalt preserve me from trouble; thou shalt compass me about with songs of deliverance." When Marley quoted that scripture, the tears began to flow down my cheeks. Such a sweet peace came over me because I felt God was telling me that there would be (songs of deliverance) from this situation and our child would be home again. About three weeks later I received a phone call from their grandmother. She said our child had contacted them and wanted to come and live with them. She wanted to make sure it was OK with us. I told her if that kid was not going to be at home with us they were the next choice of people I would want them to be with. Two weeks later our child called me and asked if they could come home. Of course I said yes. I told them I would send a bus ticket. They then proceeded to tell me, if they came home though, they wanted to be allowed to do some things. When I asked, what things, they began to name off ungodly things that had never been allowed in our home. While they were naming off the things on their list, I laid on the bed silently crying, begging God to give me wisdom on how to respond. Because, I never wanted them to be able to tell people that we would not let them come home. Though, on the other hand I could not let them dictate to us. If God ever spoke through me, he did that night. Once they finished with the list, I simply asked "has any of those things ever been a part of our home?" They replied "no". I then said "Honey, when you come home, you will come home to the home that you've always known, a home that doesn't have those things in it." It was silent on the other end of the phone line for a few moments. Then, they replied, "well, that stuff doesn't mean that much anyway." The next day I sent a bus ticket. They came home, prayed through, went back to school, graduated with their class, and went back to work. What a change!!! God has done great things in their life. ("BUT GOD"!!!) Our savior is waiting with open arms to welcome back anyone who has strayed, there's nothing you can do to make him stop loving you. If you have a child who's gone astray, don't give up. God hears your prayers!!!

When our daughter Shanna was a teenager she got a spot on the side of her face close to her temple. The spot began to grow. When I took her to the doctor he thought it might be cancer and sent it for a biopsy. Preliminary test didn't come back good. We had prayer and asked everyone we knew to pray. The next test came back negative and the spot went completely away. ("But God!!!")

Another miracle while living in Levelland was when I was working at the bank. Brad received a notice to appear in court about an increase in his child support payments. He went to court and the judge told him we had to start paying an ADDITIONAL $300 per month in child support. We were devastated. We were barely scraping by as it was. Brad was so upset and ready to give up. We went to church that night. There was a visiting evangelist. As he preached, he walked back to the pew we were sitting on. He laid his hand on Brads shoulder and said "Brother, I see the number 3. I have no idea if it is $300, $3000 or what. But, God told me to tell you that it's going to be ok. He will provide. We both broke down and began to worship the Lord. I worked at the bank at the time and another bank had just bought us out. As a result our jobs were re-evaluated and some were due a raise. As we left church that night I told Brad, perhaps I would get a $300 raise. He said "there's no way. No one gets that big a raise." A couple days later my boss called me in and told me I was getting a $300 raise. (BUT GOD!!!) He is our provider! God has been so good to us.

I worked at the Bank for about eight years. I had three week's vacation and took two of those weeks to take the kids to the youth camps and camp meetings. I took the other week to do a little family vacation each year. I wanted to make sure that my children were able to be with other children at the camp and youth camp, so I worked there in order to pay for their stay. They made lifelong friends. I am so thankful for those years. Life was never easy but it was good. I loved having our little family and our church family.

Our Shanna met our now son-in-law Greg at youth camp. He is like a Son to us. He would drive three hours from Amarillo every Friday afternoon. He would spend the weekend, wake up early Monday morning and drive home in time for college. They dated about a year and then married. It was very hard to have Shanna move three hours away, when they married. But, I knew he loved her and his family loved her and that she was in good hands. We visited them often and they visited us often. Many times they would not even tell us they were coming and would surprise us and walk in the house. She got a job with a doctor there and he worked for Payless Company and helped his grandfather in the church. His grandfather was the pastor. They both continued their college education also.

After a few years God called Shanna and Greg to Brownsville, Texas to help in ministry there. It was so hard seeing them move so far away. But, I knew they were in God's will and I would never stand in the way. I gave them all my support and blessings. While they were living in Amarillo they had a three bedroom, two bath, brick home, great jobs and great church. They lived very comfortable. I was so happy to see God's blessings on them.

When they moved to Brownsville they started out as youth leader for the church there. During the transition Shanna found out she was expecting our first Granddaughter Haley. Oh my! What excitement. We were going to be Grandparents. It was even harder to see them go. But, I knew God had great things in store for them.

My heart broke the first time I visited them in Brownsville. They were in a little mobile home that needed many repairs, on the church property. Shanna had to drive an hour each way to work and her legs and feet would swell something horrible with the pregnancy. I wanted to cry. But, I knew God was setting them up for great things and they would be blessed for the sacrifices made. They completely gave of themselves in the ministry of God.

Within just a couple years or so, the Pastor there was called to pastor somewhere else and Shanna and Greg were voted in as Pastor and First Lady. ("But God"!!!) He has blessed them tremendously. They have a wonderful church that loves them and treats them so good. They love their saints so much. God has blessed them with a beautiful home and life. He continues to bless them. I know because of the sacrifices they made when they first moved there that God is blessing them now.

Our Haley was born and changed our lives forever. There were a few complications ("But God!!!") Oh, the joy of being a grandparent. Just like with my kids, I felt I could not love anything anymore than her. What joy she brought. She was the sweetest little thing. All sass and so much fun.

Four years later our Ryan was born and I realized once again that my heart could hold more love than I ever thought possible. Before Ryan was born, medical test showed he had several medical issues. The issues were so bad that the doctors suggested Shanna have an abortion. She immediately called me and others with prayer request. Our families began to pray. One Sunday night Shanna and Greg had a visiting evangelist at their church. The evangelist knew nothing about the pregnancy or what the doctors had told Shanna. They had a wonderful service and the evangelist invited those needing a miracle to the altar. When he prayed for Shanna he told her God spoke to him and told him to tell her not to believe the doctors reports. He told her God said he had everything under control and everything was going to be ok. That same night she called me to tell me about it. While we were on the phone, Kerri called. When I switched over to talk to Kerri she told me that they had just had special prayer for Shanna and Ryan and God told her Pastor to tell all of us to stop worrying because everything was fine. I switched back over to tell Shanna and we all had a Holy Ghost hoe down. ("But God"!!!) Whatever the need, God can take care of it. When Ryan was born there were complications with his lungs. Other than that he was a perfectly healthy baby that we all doted on. He was in the hospital for six weeks. Talk about rejoicing when we brought him home. He was the cutest thing and such a joy. My heart was filled to the brim.

Brownsville was 8 hours from where we lived. I had to see my kids and grandbabies though. So, I've made that trip often. Every time Shanna and Greg needed to be out of town for a conference or meeting or whatever, I would travel down and stay with the kids. Oh, what mischief we would get into. So many wonderful memories. I would travel with Shanna and Greg many times to camps and keep Haley and Ryan in the hotel rooms because they were still too young to be in class. We made some wonderful memories. Thankfully, even though Shanna and Greg lived farther away, they still came to see us often, as well. They have pastored in Brownsville for over 20 years now. I'm so thankful for all God has done and I'm so very proud of them. Our Haley just graduated from Indiana Bible College and Ryan just graduated from high school and is attending Indiana Bible College.

Just a year or so after Shanna and Greg married, Kerri went off to Jackson Bible college, in Jackson Mississippi. I drove her to Mississippi to check out the college. We had a great trip. As a mother my heart was aching and did not want to let her go that far away. However, I knew it was God's will and that was where she needed to be. That is one of the best things that ever happened in her life. She met Chris there and they eventually married. They were married about 7 years and had our Keaton. Once again my heart was over the moon with love for that little guy. He cried a lot and when we took him to the doctor they found out that somehow his collar bone was broken during the delivery. Oh how my heart hurt for him. But, he healed quickly and soon became a joyful, rambunctious bundle of joy. Once again my heart held love more than I could imagine. Then 17 months later our Kaysen was born. He was so adorable and loved to be cuddled. This Nanas heart felt like it would burst wide open with love. It wasn't easy for Kerri, having two so close together. Chris and Kerri settled in Vicksburg ,MS. I traveled up and down the road all the time to be with them and they traveled to our house in between. When the boys started school they would come and stay a week every summer and spring break. I would go keep the boys so Chris and Kerri could get away also. So many great memories were made. Chris and Kerri were married over 10 years. But, as with many couples they had some problems that could not be resolved, and consequently lead to divorce. My heart broke for both of them. I worried so much about Kerri and the boys. I spent as much time as I could with them. ("But God"!!!). A year or so later Kerri met our now Son-in-law Steve. Steve quickly became part of our family and we grew close. Like our other SIL, he's like a Son to us. He has helped us in so many ways. We thank God for all he has done.

After Shanna and Greg married and Kerri went off to college, our Son, Marley, was suddenly an only child. Poor guy, he didn't know quite how to handle all that. Quite frankly neither did Brad and I. So there were some adjustments. One day during a routine check up for Marley the doctor found an issue and said they needed to do immediate surgery and additional test because in most cases like his, it was almost always leukemia. The doctor said Marley had to have surgery to repair the problem. Those words were so scary. We immediately sent out prayer request and touched the throne of God. Doctors performed the surgery to repair the problem and did additional test. Our savior once again performed a miracle. Additional test came back, No Leukemia. ("BUT GOD!!!") I praise him for the healing of our Son. Marley's recovery from that surgery caused him to miss several weeks of school. Then, a few short months later I woke him up to get ready for school and when he started to get out of bed he told me he could not move his legs. What a scary thing to hear from your child. I was able to rent a wheelchair. Took him to the doctor and he was immediately hospitalized. He had a rare muscle infection that only about 2000 people in the world get. ("But God"!!!) His healing power was already at work in Marley's body. Marley was in the hospital for a week, and consequently out of school another couple weeks. By then he had missed so much school he was pretty much out of the loop on everything.

I was still working at the bank at that time and had been there several years. I felt like Marley needed more one on one. I began to fast and pray that God would open the doors for me to open an in-home daycare again so that I could home school him and still bring home an income.

Bank One had just bought out our small town bank. One day an announcement came across our desk that there was a mandatory, very important meeting at the close of business. All employees were instructed to meet in the conference room upstairs. In that meeting we were told that the new bank said they had to let at least four people go. They did not feel they could let anyone go. So, they left the decision up to the employees. Our bank manager said if there was any of us that were looking at another career, wanted to go back to school or anything else, this might be a great opportunity. They said we would be offered a severance pay, our vacation pay, plus it would be looked upon as a lay off so we could draw six months of unemployment. I was so excited. This was my answer to prayer. As soon as the meeting was over I met with the manager and my supervisor. I explained to them how I had been praying and I felt this was an answer to my prayer. My supervisor told me that out of everyone in the bank I was the last person she would've thought of. She said they didn't know what they would do without me. But, they understood. So, within a couple weeks I quit working at the bank. With the benefits package the bank offered, I was able to buy a little single wide mobile home to put in the back of our house as an attachment to use as a daycare. I took all the necessary courses and got the licenses required. However, before opening the daycare I took a few months off. We took a long vacation. Then I opened the daycare and began to home school Marley.

("BUT GOD"!!!) Once again my prayers were answered. I had the day care for a couple years. Then, our church split and we found ourselves without a Pastor. God started dealing with us about moving somewhere else.

Brad's best friend Jimmy Brumley was managing the auto department of a Montgomery Wards store. They were transferring him to a little town called Belton, Texas. Jimmy called Brad and asked him to be his assistant manager. Belton was a beautiful little town with a gorgeous lake. We prayed about it and felt the release to go. We started preparing to move. Brad turned in his notice at his job. I gave notice to all my Day Care families and put a for sale sign on our property. Then suddenly Jimmy's transfer to Belton, fell through. He was being transferred to Fort Worth, Texas instead. He called Brad and told him he still wanted him to be his assistant manager but it would be in Fort Worth. At that point there wasn't much we could do but accept the job. So, we talked it over and decided to move to Fort Worth. Brad moved there first and stayed with friends. While Marley and I stayed in Levelland until our land sold. We would meet Brad halfway on the weekends to spend time together. Within a couple months our land sold and the movers came to move our double wide mobile home. While our home was being set up we had to stay with the Brumleys a couple weeks. Of course we went to church with them. So, by the time we moved into our home Marley had already become a part of the youth group. As a result we did not have the heart to change churches. Even though it was a 30 minute drive both ways in the horrible Fort Worth traffic. We loved the church but it sure took us a while to adjust to big city life. Before long we were singing in the choir, helping with Sunday school, and coached the quiz team. The Euless church had never had a quiz team. The kids were eager to learn. We actually had so many young people we had three teams. We won several team trophies and the kids won individual trophies and ribbons. What a joy it was to see the kids desire to learn Gods word. We had many great and fun quiz trips to different tournaments.

I worked at the bank for a short time and Brad worked for a welding company. After a few month's people in church found out I previously had a daycare and asked me to keep their kids. So, I gave my notice at the bank and started in home daycare.

One day in the middle of the day I heard a noise at the front door. I opened it up and there was Brad crawling up the steps. He had hurt his back on the job. Long story short he was off work for a year. He drew disability through his job. However child-support took a substantial amount out of his check each month, so his check was only about $600 a month. I brought in about $1000 a month. We struggled but God helped us through that trying time. ("But God!!!) He is our provider. Through the disability program Brad went back to school to get his GED so he could find a job he could do with his back injury. He could not stand any length of time. So, it had to be a sit down job. There were only two jobs offered in that genre. One was working at a desk using a computer and the other was driving a truck. Brad chose to become a truck driver. He went to work for Tarrant concrete and worked there for 20+ years. ("But God"!!!). Although Brad hurting his back and being on disability for a year was horrible it wound up being for the good. During that year he was able to get his GED, which he had always wanted to do. Also, with the truck driver training and licensing he made more money than he had ever made. What a blessing.

We lived in Fort Worth a little over two years when I was in a serious car accident. I was on my way to the church to speak to a group about soul winning. Traffic was at a standstill and a lady rear ended me going about 70 miles an hour. Her car shoved me into the car in front of me which started a chain reaction. The impact knocked me out. When I regained consciousness, my car was smoking and people were at my door trying to get it open to get me out. An ambulance arrived shortly and took me to the hospital. Our dog, Watson, was in the car with me. The impact threw him in the floor but he seemed to be OK. Of course he was protecting me. So, he was barking and snapping at everyone trying to help me. An EMT put on a pair of thick gloves, picked Watson up, and calmed him down. Then he let him ride in the ambulance sitting in his lap. I will never forget that act of kindness. Someone ask for my phone and called my husband and son to let them know what happened and which hospital the ambulance was taking me to. Once we arrived at the hospital I was immediately checked for internal bleeding, broken bones and so on. When I was taken back to my room the doctor came in and said "you must be a popular lady, because that waiting room is filled with Pentecostals." Our Son knew people were waiting for me at the church so he went there to let them know I wouldn't make it. So, as soon as they heard about it they all came to the hospital.

That accident did lots of damage. I have several herniated, protruding and bulging disc in my lumbar and my cervical spine. I have fibromyalgia from the nerve, muscle and ligament damage. There are times I'm in so much pain I want to cry. ("BUT GOD!!!") He gives me strength beyond my understanding and I'm alive!!! Unfortunately I have not been able to hold down a full-time job since then. However, God has given me the strength and the stability to do jobs on my good days. He always supplies our every need.

There was a positive to that accident though. We got a little settlement and was able to pay our mobile home off, take a vacation and a few other things. Also, I was able to start drawing Social Security disability, which was almost as much money as I was bringing home before the accident. It allowed me to be able to go to Brownsville and Mississippi to help my girls when I was needed. It helped me to be there when their babies were born, to be there to take care of the kids while they took some much-needed time off and so on. I was able to go to camp with Shanna and Greg and keep the kids while they were working the camps. Although it was a bad accident, I still count it as a blessing, because I would have never been able to see my kids and grand babies as often as I do, and did back then. ("BUT GOD"!!!) God has been so good to us and he knows the desires of our heart. After that accident things finally started coming together in Fort Worth and life was good.

We started a bus ministry. We called it Sunday School Evangelism. About 30 people joined the team. We would go to a different apartment complex each month and have games, clowns, balloons and so on. Then we would tell the crowd about Jesus and invite them to church. God moved miraculously. It wasn't long before we needed more buses. Some parents rode the bus with their kids and several were saved and have been part of the church for many years now. ("But God"!!!") He answered our prayers that the Sunday School Evangelism Team would reach many souls. I love working for the Lord and telling others about Jesus. I'm so thankful for all he did during that time.

As time went on Marley met a beautiful girl at youth camp, who eventually became our daughter-in-law. We were so happy for him that he had found a good Christian girl. We grew to love Mandy like a daughter. She has been such a blessing. She truly is a daughter to me. She and I have developed a bond that not many mother and daughter-in-law have. Although we were thrilled for Marley and

Mandy it didn't make it any easier for our youngest child to be leaving home. The empty nest syndrome set in and it was very hard. Brad and I learned to handle not having any kids in the house.

Seven years or so later Marley and Mandy had their first child, our fifth grandchild, Shelby, who became such a part of our lives. Oh my goodness, that beautiful baby girl squeezed herself right into my heart. I can't begin to explain what joy it was to have a baby around again. God used her to mend so much in our lives. There are no words to explain the love I felt for her. Just like our other four. Then about four years later Cooper came along. He was the cutest bundle of joy. Once again my heart opened completely up and overflowed with love for this amazing little guy. Then 17 months later Bodie Ray arrived. Those blue eyes and curly, red hair captured my heart. Like all the other Grandkids he has brought unbelievable joy and the love I have for him is just like the previous 6 Grand blessings.

July 2009 I suffered a heart attack. I had three heart stents placed. All our kids gathered around us and gave us great support. Everyone went home once they found I was ok, except Shanna and Greg. They brought me home from the hospital and stayed several days. When I was released from the hospital I was told to return to the hospital immediately if I had any chest pain. I awoke the next morning having chest pains so Shanna and Greg insisted they take me back to emergency. Once there I was hospitalized and another stent placed. The next afternoon the nurse told me he was going to give me a shot of Demerol to help me sleep. As soon as that shot hit my veins I knew something was wrong. I hollered for the nurse but they didn't hear me. Then I told Shanna something was wrong and asked her to pray. I then lost consciousness. When I awoke 4 hours later my room was full of family again. Shanna said when I passed out, all kinds of alarms started going off. She said about every doctor and nurse on that hospital ward was at my bedside. My heart rate went over 200. I had a bad allergic reaction. ("But God") he kept his hand on me. From that point on (highly allergic to Demerol) is in my medical chart. I was released a couple days later. Shanna stayed at the house with me for two weeks, then went home. After she left, my body began to absorb all the new heart meds the doctor had put me on. I was sick as a dog. I was very scared I was going to have another heart attack and no one be at home to help me. So, I left the house as soon as possible every day and would go to McDonalds with a notebook, ink pen and highlighter in hand. I would research the medications I was on to see if I could find out why I felt so bad. I found I was not supposed to take a couple drugs together. As I figured out my meds and talked with my cardiologist, I began to feel better. It took me about two years to feel normal again ("But God!!!") He calmed my fear and I was able to carry on. I continue to watch what I eat and exercise an hour a day, as much as possible. I went several years without another blockage but in 2016 I had another one and a stent placed. Then in 2018 I had a sixth stent placed. Just recently I was feeling bad. So, I went to the doctor. They did and angiogram and found I had built up scar tissue inside one of my stents. My cardiologist tried to balloon it but that didn't work. So, he referred me to an interventional cardiologist who along with an oncologist went in and did radiation to remove the scar tissue blockage. ("But God"!!!) That was so scary but he guided both physician's hands and everything is ok. Praise his holy name. I asked the doctors why I keep having blockages when I watch my diet, exercise and do everything they tell me to do, to the best of my ability. They said that it is genetic. They told me I would be a lot worse off if I didn't do those things. I'm trusting my Lord and praying I have no more blockages.

Throughout the past 10 years several loved ones that I've mentioned in this book have passed away. All my Grandparents passed away many years ago. In the past 10 years Mom Helms, Dad Helms, my paternal Dad, my stepmother, mother-in-law, father-in-law, both my sisters, aunts, uncles, my Mom and several others have gone on to their eternal reward. There was so much grief when each one passed.

My sister Tina and I had never been close. She was as wild as you can get. She participated in about every sinful thing there is. She used drugs and alcohol. For a while she belonged to a wild Hells Angels type motorcycle gang and was downright mean. We loved each other but we were miles apart in every way. When I had my heart attack she called my youngest sister Jacque and told her she felt an urgent need to come visit me. She also said she wanted to go to church with me and receive the Holy Ghost while she was at my house. So, Tina and Jacque both came to visit for a week. We had a great time. They went to church with me and were saved. ("But God!!!") The prayers I had prayed for their salvation had been answered. I'm so thankful they found the Lord. From that point, Tina and I talked every day. We became very close. Tina had a major transformation. God did a great work in her life. Then, about a year later she was at Moms house. She reached to get a French fries from the table, became faint and suddenly dropped to the floor. My Brother did CPR but she was gone by the time the ambulance got there. She passed away November 7, 2010. Coroner said it was a massive heart attack. We were devastated. I am so thankful she was saved and for the relationship we had developed. I miss her every day. ("But God"!!!) He wipes away every tear. He wraps his arms of peace and comfort around us.

My sister Jacque passed away 5 years later in May of 2015. Jacque had once been a very devout Christian. She backslid and went deep into sin. However, we talked nearly every day. Jacque had become very mentally unstable. She had lots of treatments. As long as she stayed on her medication she was somewhat normal, but I always knew the minute she had stopped taking her meds. When I saw her number show up on my caller ID I would brace myself. Because, I never knew if when I answered the phone, she would be telling me how much she loved me and how she didn't know what she would do without me. How she told everyone I was not only her sister, but her mother, best friend, counselor, etc. Or, if she would be cussing me out, telling me she hated me and had hired a hit man to kill me, because she found out I talked to her estranged daughter or some other crazy reason. The last time I saw her was when her husband Warren passed away. I went to stay with her a few days because I knew she had no one else. When I got home from the funeral I tried calling her to check how she was doing. She had called and left a very nasty message on my phone. I tried for a couple weeks to reach her. Then I asked my cousin to go check on her. He had the police go with him. Sadly they found her partially decomposed body on the floor, with her legs underneath the refrigerator door. The coroner said she had passed away about 10 days earlier. From what I understand she took her medication wrong, possibly with alcohol that caused a coronary event. My heart aches every time I think about it. I pray she had time to make things right with God. I miss her terribly. ("But God"!!!) He is our peace.

My Mom got a disease called Bullous Pemphigoid. It was a disease where a little tiny blister would come up on her skin and then it would grow to the size of a grapefruit. The blister would be full of fluid and then burst. Once it burst it left raw exposed skin. This was all over her body. She looked like a burn victim. She could not stand for anything to touch her. I went to California to try to find doctors and hospitals that could help her. However, the disease was so rare no one knew what to do for it. I got her into a hospital we thought would help. But, they just did not know how to treat the disease. It broke my heart to see her suffer like that. She passed away two years after Jacque did on March 23, 2017. I hated seeing her suffer the way she did. But, I knew she had made things right with God and was in a better place. No more suffering, no more pain. Many years before she passed she made things right with me. She said she realized, in later years that she needed psychiatric help during those abusive years. I knew that was her way of apologizing. She never did come out and say she was sorry, but I knew she was. Many years before her passing we had become close. I called her every Wednesday night on my way home from church. Mom did not know how to show love but she tried in her own way. She took us girls on a girl trip a few years before she passed away. I will never forget it. We made her a memory book of the trip. There is some hilarious stuff in that book. A few years ago she asked me to take her to her 67th high school reunion. It was just she and I for the first time. We had a great trip and I will always treasure the memories of that trip.

My mother-in-law passed away on September 10, 2013. We were very close. She had Alzheimer's. But, when I called her at the hospital in California she would ask how things were in Texas and beg me to come and get her. It broke my heart to not be able to drive out there and bring her home. The nurse was always surprised that she could just tell her, Debbie was on the phone and she knew immediately who it was. She had a true walk with God and although my heart broke when she left this world, I knew she was in a far better one.

("But God!!!") He truly is our comforter. I know I will see them again someday.

A SECOND CHANCE AT LIFE

 t first it may seem like gloom and doom, but if you keep reading you will see the miracles.

On March 26, 2019 (Bradley Robinson) my husband went in to the hospital for double bypass surgery. The surgery went well and he was recovering well. The surgery was on a Tuesday. By Friday he was up walking around with a walker. The medical team was happy with his progress and we were supposed to be released and going home on Sunday. However, Brad was developing pneumonia and was coughing profusely. On Friday night, in the middle of the night he coughed while sleeping. Then he let out a blood curdling scream and began to moan and groan. He cried out in pain throughout the night, saying he could feel something moving and stabbing him. I begged the medical team to help him. I asked them to give him more pain meds or whatever it took to relieve his suffering. They told me they were giving him the maximum pain cocktail. The strongest most potent there was. No one could figure out why he was in so much pain.

The surgeon came in around 10:00 AM the next morning. It was Saturday. He could hear Brads screams down the hall. He walked into our room, patted Brads arm and told him to calm down. Then he motioned for me to come into the hallway and told me to go in by Brad's bedside and rub his head and arm and tell him to calm down. He then told me that he thought Brad had probably busted a wire, used to attach the sternum. At that point I asked him if they were going to go back in and repair the wire or what were they going to do about it. The surgeon said they were not going to do anything because of the risk involved. Then he turned around and started doing something on the computer. I could hear Brad crying out in pain as I stood in the hall. So, when the surgeon turned back around, I asked him if Brad was going to have to live like that, the rest of his life. The surgeon then threw his hands in the air and said (in a very stern voice) "so we are back to the wire again. I thought we were done with the wire". He said "I have a floor full of patients that have had the same surgery and none of them are acting this way. He indicated Brad was over reacting. Then he left.

I was so distraught. I went back in the room and videoed Brad writhing in pain. I sent the video to our kids and asked them if they thought it looked like he was over reacting. (They had all gone home a day or two before, because Brad was doing so well.) They could not believe it. Our Son immediately headed for the hospital.

At 3:00 PM that same day Brads body could not take the pain any longer. He had his first seizure and his body began to shut down. Also, there was lots of blood seeping through his incision and through his hospital gown by then. Still nothing was being done to see what was going on. He had two more seizures that evening. Around 11:00 PM the night nurse in charge, called the surgeon and said "if we don't do something for this man he's going to die." At that point the surgeon told them to put Brad back on the ventilator. The next morning, (which was now Sunday morning) the day nurse called the surgeon and said "Brad is still coughing profusely, even though he is back on the ventilator."

FINALLY, after more than 20 hours of Brad suffering, moaning and groaning, telling everyone something was stabbing him, the surgeon finally said "OK, there really is something wrong then." He then told the medical team to put Brad in a medically induced coma so he couldn't cough anymore and do anymore damage internally. The next day (Monday) they finally did X-rays, which showed when Brad coughed so hard Friday night, he literally busted open his sternum. All the wires the doctors used to reattach his sternum after the surgery, had come loose. X-rays showed that every time Brad moved, coughed, swallowed or anything, those wires would saw into his sternum bones. They immediately took him in for surgery to repair everything that had busted open. They said the wires that had been wrapped around his sternum looked like a tangled up fishing line. They showed me the X-ray that looked like someone had taken a tiny saw and sawed each bone. A lung had also herniated, which is so rare most doctors have never heard of it.

Brad never came out of that third seizure on Saturday night and when they brought him back Monday after the repair surgery he just would not come out of the coma. Then every organ in his body began to shut down. His brain, lungs, stomach, kidneys, nerves, muscles and everything else shut down. He was on 24 hours a day dialysis, a stomach tube was placed, a tracheostomy was performed and a tracheostomy tube put in his throat. He had many blood transfusions. His blood sugar went crazy so he was on high doses of insulin. He had never been diabetic before. As each organ shut down the doctors would have a conference with me and I would have to sign for each procedure to be done. Each time when they walked out of the room I would say ("But God"!!!)

In the middle of everything going on, I started having chest pains. My daughter took me to emergency in the same hospital. While in the ER the nephrologist came in my room with papers to sign, so they could start dialysis on Brad. When they had me sign for the dialysis, they told me that he more than likely would be on dialysis the rest of his life. I looked at those around me and said ("BUT GOD"!!!)

The ER doctor wound up admitting me into the heart hospital on the same floor Brad was on. As soon as I was settled in my hospital room the nurse let me go see Brad. Although he was still in a coma I wanted him to feel my presence. We were with him pretty much 24/7.

My girls, Shanna and Kerri, stayed in my hospital room with me. They tried to sleep in a couple recliners that would literally shoot across the room when they tried to recline. We laughed so hard that night. I told them God knew we needed the laugh. Thankfully the chest pains were not from a heart attack. I had low potassium and gallbladder issues. But, since I have 6 heart stints, they wanted to evaluate me over night. I was released the next day and went straight to Brads room. ("But God"!!!)

Nearly every day there was something scary that would happen with Brad. One day they came running into the waiting room and told us Brad was crashing and they needed me to sign papers to use the crash cart on him. They said he could die. After signing the papers, me and my family began to call on Jesus and I said ("But God"!!!!)

When they had me sign to have the trach put in I was told he may have it the rest of his life. They said if he did, he would only be able to have food intravenously the rest of his life. I walked out of the room and said ("BUT GOD"!!!!)

When they put the stomach tube in, again, I was told it may never come out. I then said ("BUT GOD"!!!!)

When our kids and I walked into the room and saw the surgeon sitting by Brads bed with his head down and then told us he had never seen anything like this before and unfortunately they didn't know what else to do. Brad should have awakened by then. With tears in my eyes I walked out of that room saying ("BUT GOD"!!!)

When they told me that if he did wake up he might be in a vegetative state or he would probably be like a baby. He may have to learn to feed himself, dress himself and so on. I said ("BUT GOD"!!!) Each time I was told bad news I would declare ("But God!!!")

People from our church, all our kids churches as well as family and friends all over the world were praying. Brads room was filled daily with friends and family laying hands on him, praying. So many people would come and sit with us in the waiting room for hours to keep us company.

After seven weeks in a coma the medical team told me they had exhausted every possible thing they knew to do for Brad. So he was being transferred to a Long Term Acute Critical Care Hospital. They handed me some pamphlets and asked me to let them know which LTACH I wanted him transferred to. At that point, I admit my faith wavered a little. My kids (who had been with me nonstop, and such a source of strength, had all just left the hospital. So, when I was given the news and told to find an LTACH I was alone. I went into the waiting room, which had pretty much become home, and broke down. I cried out to God and his sweet presence filled that place. ("BUT GOD")!!! I could feel his arms around me.

Brad was moved to an LTACH facility by ambulance within a couple days. It was a scary time. There were only 5 ICU beds in a very small room. Each bed was behind a curtain and very little room for visitors. Up until then I was with Brad pretty much 24/7, but, at the LTACH even family had very strict visiting hours. The doctors and nurses there, said it was because they needed to concentrate on getting my husband off the ventilator, out of the coma and well. There were a lot of ups and downs the 6 weeks he was in LTACH. Brad would make progress and then digress. During my allowed visitations (every 2 hours) I would lay hands on the medical equipment, the bed, the IV's and all over Brad, pleading the blood.

During the sixth week in LTACH he came out of his coma. ("But God"!!!) Within the week he was completely off dialysis. It took a while for him to be weaned off the ventilator. He would go a few hours and be ok. Then the medical team would have to put him back on it. This went on for several days. But, finally the day came when he was able to be off it indefinitely. The trach was eventually removed with no complications. The stomach tube wasn't taken out immediately, but within just a few days Brad was able to eat and digest normally. The doctors could not believe it. He held the spoon and did not have to learn like a baby. The first time they got him up his legs were just like wet noodles. He could not support himself, even with a walker. But with therapy he got stronger every day. ("But God"!!!) He performed miracle, after miracle.

We were then transferred to a rehabilitation hospital for several weeks where he learned to walk with a walker and do simple mental/cognitive tasks. After 3 months of hospitals we finally got to go home. Then we had outpatient therapy every single day for an additional 3 months. By the end of September 2019 Brad was walking without assistance. ("But God"!!!)

The miracles and testimony continues. Brad had a full time job until all of this. So, suddenly there was no weekly check. I don't remember mentioning that to anyone. We had some savings to fall back on. However, God used his people miraculously. I can't tell you the numerous people who would take my hand and put a $20, $50, or $100 in it. People would say "Debbie, you're a giver. We know it's hard for you to take, but take this." Our church blessed us unbelievably, our neighbor took it upon herself to set up a "Go fund me."

Once we were home, our church ladies brought food for days and days. It was unbelievable.

Long term disability denied our claim. Saying Brad's illness was pre-existing. I had to prove to them that the herniated lung, pneumonia and other issues happened in the hospital, not before. So, still no check, ("But God"!!!) Suddenly, out of the blue, we began receiving a monthly check from someone we had not heard from in over 40 years. They did not know our financial situation but, they said God told them to send a check for six months. We were flabbergasted. Close to the end of the year Brad's disability was approved. The person sending the monthly checks did not know that we had received the letter saying he was approved. However, he called us and told us that he was letting us know that he was sending the last check. God had told him. What a great big God we serve. Those checks ended the same month the LTD checks began. ("But God"!!!") He is our Jehovah Jireh. Our provider.

Brad had not been home from the hospital very long when I started having major stomach/digestive issues. I went to the doctor and preliminary test were done. To my dismay, the test came back positive for cancer. That was all I needed. I was still having to take Brad to therapy every day. However, a colonoscopy was scheduled. I was so scared and distraught. To be frank, I was a basket case. Once again I reached out to friends and family for prayer. We bound together and touched the throne of God. The results of the colonoscopy and other tests showed I had an ulcer, diverticulitis and a couple other things that could be treated with medication. Six polyps were removed and sent in for results. The polyps were pre-cancerous, but no current cancer. ("But God"!!!) What a relief. I have to have a colonoscopy every three years now. But, that's OK. I recently had one since it's been 3 years. There were no polyps and everything looked great. ("But God"!!!)

2019 will be a year forever in our memory. Brad still has some issues, bad neuropathy throughout, and that herniated lung has doctors completely baffled. People who did not know him before cannot believe what he went through. He now works part time in the mornings at a little grocery store and people love him. Little old ladies give him tips all the time for carrying out their groceries for them. He mows the lawn and weed eats. It is unbelievable the things he can do. ("BUT GOD"!!!) Just look at what he's done.

Our daughter and Son-in-law offered us a place close to them, with a country setting and quite life style.. We first talked to our Pastors, then our other kids. They supported the move 100%.

One of the hardest things I ever did was having to tell our 7 year old granddaughter Shelby that we we're moving. My heart broke as the tears flowed down her cheeks. I promised her I would try to visit at least once a month. Thankfully God has made a way and for the most part I've been able to keep that promise.

So, in December of 2019 all our kids and grandkids moved us from Texas, to Louisiana. Kerri, Steve and the boys have been so good to us and our Pastor Trusley, First Lady and church are amazing.

There have been some challenges but like always God has seen us through. The biggest challenge is being so far from our other kids and Grandkids and Texas friends. Although I love being close to our kids and Grandkids here. I'm thankful for Face Time.

We continue to have financial challenges but through every trial and test, God has been so faithful. We see him everywhere. Brads disability checks ended last year, June 8, 2021. It's not as easy financially as we would like ("But God"!!!). He supplies our every need.

I want to once again thank God, our kids and grandkids who have been a source of strength as they walked this road with us. I truly don't know what I would have done without them. Our daughters Shanna and Kerri made many trips and stayed weeks at a time with me. Our Son, Marley drove up often as soon as he got off work and stayed hours. Their spouses and kids came with them as often as they could. I was very seldom alone. I thank Pastor and Sis Benson, for their numerous visits to the hospital and support, Pastor Mclaughlin, the Euless Church and all our friends and neighbors for their unwavering outpouring of love and support. We would not have made it through without them. We are so thankful for each one. May God pour many blessings upon them.

I hope this blesses someone. Just remember, the media, doctors and anyone else may paint a scary picture of whatever is going on in your life. ("BUT GOD"!!!)

Louisiana

As I previously said, we moved to Louisiana December 28, 2019. All our kids and grandkids moved us in during a torrential rain. There was mud everywhere. After a long trip from Texas everyone was exhausted but so sweet. Those who could, stayed for several days to help us get things organized.

The first couple months of 2020 were spent getting our house, doctors and all that comes with a move put in order. In March we were finally ready to start inviting people from our church over so we could get acquainted. Then a horrible virus, Covid 19, swept throughout the United States and other countries. Thousands died from it. We had to be careful, social distance, and wear mask. Marley, Mandy, Cooper, Steve, Kerri, Keaton and Kaysen have all had it. Some of them were hospitalized. ("But God!!!") he brought them through it. Besides still having issues with taste they have recovered.

Brad and I were vaccinated and try to follow all safety guidelines. There is so much controversy among people. When it comes to vaccines, mask, social distancing. But, I know, just like everything else in my life, my God will be with me and my family. I pray a hedge of protection around each one.

In September 2021, for the first time we had to evacuate, due to a hurricane. Hurricane IDA caused much destruction. Our power was out for several days. Thankfully we left and went to Marley and Mandy's before the storm. Once our power was back on we came home. The high winds had blown some of our siding off. Also, our mobile home skirting was bent and blown under our home and some shingles blown off and broken. Food in our refrigerator was ruined. We are so thankful that was the extent of damage and things were not worse. ("But God"!!!) He kept his hand on Steve, Kerri and the boys, plus other family and friends and no one was harmed.

As I close this book I give all honor, glory and praise to my God and thank him for all he's done for me and my family. I do not know what the future holds, but I know who holds the future. I know that whatever comes my way, my God will be there. He will hold my hand and walk with me every step of the way. He is my comfort, my peace, my joy, my healer, my provider, my victory, my savior and so much more.

I pray this book is an encouragement and lets those who read it know that no matter what you are going through, there is power in the blood of Jesus, you can make it. Keep holding onto Jesus he can turn your darkest hours into light and your life can be beautiful!

God Bless You
Debbie Robinson

CPSIA information can be obtained
at www.ICGtesting.com
Printed in the USA
LVHW080055190822
726215LV00012B/297